Mike McGrath

Coding for Beginners

In easy steps is an imprint of In Easy Steps Limited
16 Hamilton Terrace · Holly Walk · Leamington Spa
Warwickshire · United Kingdom · CV32 4LY
www.ineasysteps.com

Notice of Liability
Every effort has been made to ensure that this book contains accurate
and current information. However, In Easy Steps Limited and the
author shall not be liable for any loss or damage suffered by readers
as a result of any information contained herein.

Trademarks
All trademarks are acknowledged as belonging to their respective
companies.

In Easy Steps Limited supports The Forest Stewardship Council (FSC),
the leading international forest certification organisation. All our titles
that are printed on Greenpeace approved FSC certified paper carry the
FSC logo.

MIX
Paper from
responsible sources
FSC   FSC® C020837
www.fsc.org

LONDON BOROUGH OF WANDSWORTH	
9030 00005 6554 1	
Askews & Holts	17-Aug-2017
005.1	£10.99
	WW17008707

Printed and bound in the United Kingdom

ISBN 978-1-84078-642-2

Contents

Preface

The creation of this book has provided me, Mike McGrath, a welcome opportunity to produce an introduction to coding computer programs for readers with no previous coding experience. Although this is a book for beginners, it goes beyond the mere basics so some topics may be more easily understood after gaining some coding experience with the simpler listed programs. All the examples demonstrate coding features using the popular Python programming language and the book's screenshots illustrate the actual results produced by executing the listed code.

Conventions in this book

In order to clarify the code listed in the steps given in each example, I have adopted the same default colorization convention provided by Python's code editor. Keywords of the Python language itself are colored orange, built-in function names are purple, coder-specified function names are blue, text strings are green, comments are red, and all other code is black, like this:

```
# A function to display a greeting
def greet( reader ) :
    print( 'Welcome to Coding for Beginners' , reader )
```

Additionally, in order to identify each source code file described in the steps, an icon and file name appears in the margin alongside the steps, like this:

program.py

Grabbing the source code

For convenience I have placed source code files from the examples featured in this book into a single ZIP archive. You can obtain the complete archive by following these easy steps:

1. Browse to **www.ineasysteps.com** then navigate to Free Resources and choose the Downloads section

2. Find Coding for Beginners in easy steps in the list, then click on the hyperlink entitled All Code Examples to download the archive

3. Now, extract the archive contents to any convenient location on your computer

1 Getting started

Welcome to the exciting, fun world of computer coding! This chapter describes how to create your own programming environment and demonstrates how to code your very first program.

Programming code

A computer is merely a machine that can process a set of simple instructions very quickly. The set of instructions it processes is known as a "program", and the instructions are known as "code".

People who write computer programs are known as "programmers" or "coders". Their programs have enabled computers to become useful in almost every area of modern life:

- **In the hand** – computers are found in cellphone devices for tasks such as communication via voice, text, and social media

- **In the home** – computers are found in household devices such as TV sets, gaming consoles, and washing machines

- **In the office** – computers are found in desktop devices for tasks such as word processing, payroll, and graphic design

- **In the store** – computers are found in retail devices such as automatic teller machines (ATMs) and bar code scanners

- **In the car** – computers are found in control devices for tasks such as engine management, anti-lock braking and security

- **In the sky** – computers are found in airplanes for piloting and in air traffic control centers for safe navigation

These are, in fact, just a few examples of how computers affect our lives today. Yet, computers are really dumb! They can only count from zero to one, and cannot think for themselves.

A computer is a collection of electronic components – collectively known as "hardware". To make the computer function it must be given a set of program instructions – known as "software".

It is important that each computer program provides clear step-by-step instructions that the computer can execute without errors. The coder must therefore break down the task required of the computer into simple unambiguous steps. For example, a program to move a mobile robot from indoors to outdoors must include instructions to have the robot locate a doorway and navigate around any obstacles. So the coder must always consider what possible unexpected difficulties a program may encounter.

Program instructions must be presented to the computer in a language it can understand. At the most basic level the computer can understand "machine code", which moves items around in its memory to perform tasks. This type of obscure low-level code is incredibly tedious as it requires many lines of instruction to perform even a simple task.

Fortunately, over the years, many "high-level" programming languages have been developed that allow the coder to compose instructions in more human-readable form. These modern high-level programs are automatically translated into the machine code that the computer can understand by a "compiler" or by an "interpreter". In order to become a coder you must typically learn at least one of these high-level programming languages:

Programs written in an interpreted language can be run immediately but those written in compiled languages must first be compiled before they can be run.

- **C** – a powerful compiled language that is closely mapped to machine code and used to develop operating systems

- **C++** – an enhanced compiled language developing on C to provide classes for Object Oriented Programming (OOP)

- **C#** – a modern compiled language designed by Microsoft for the .NET framework and Common Language Infrastructure

- **Java** – a portable compiled language that is designed to run on any platform regardless of the hardware architecture

- **Python** – a dynamic interpreted language that allows both functional and Object Oriented Programming (OOP)

Just as human languages have similarities, such as verbs and nouns, these programming languages have certain similarities as they each possess "data structures", in which to store information, and "control structures" that determine how the program proceeds.

Python is a total package of "batteries included".

The examples in this book use the Python language to demonstrate how to code computer programs as it has a simple language syntax, requires no compilation, includes a large library of standard functions, and can be used to create both Console programs and windowed GUI (Graphical User Interface) apps.

Setting up

Before you can begin coding programs in the Python language you need to set up a programming environment on your computer, by installing the Python interpreter and the standard library of tested code modules that comes along with it. This is available online as a free download from the Python Software Foundation.

Installers for Mac OS X and other platforms are also freely available at **python.org/downloads**

1 Launch a web browser and navigate to **python.org/downloads** then click the **Download** button to grab the latest version for your system – in this case it's "Python 3.5.1"

2 When the download completes, find the executable (**.exe**) file in your Downloads folder, then **Open** Python Setup

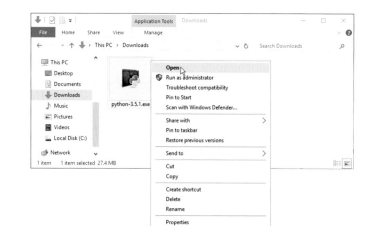

3 Next, be sure to check the Python Setup option box to select the feature to **Add Python 3.5 to PATH**

Hot tip

Adding Python to the System Path makes it available from within any directory. After installation, you can enter the exact command **python -V** at a Command Prompt to see the interpreter respond with its version number.

10

④ Now, click the Python Setup dialog's **Install Now** option to begin copying files onto your computer

Hot tip

Do accept the suggested destination directory.

⑤ Click the **Close** button to complete your Python Setup

Upon completion, the Python group is added to your Start/All Apps menu. Most important of this group is the **IDLE** item that launches the Python integrated development environment.

Hot tip

You will use the IDLE launcher often, so right-click on its icon and choose "Pin to taskbar" to make it readily available from the Windows Desktop.

Exploring IDLE

The installed Python software package includes the Integrated DeveLopment Environment (IDLE) in which you can easily code and run programs, or snippets, written in the Python language. IDLE provides two different windows for program development:

● Shell Window

● Edit Window

When you start up IDLE it opens a new window containing a menu bar, a banner describing the version, and a **>>>** prompt. This is the Shell Window in which you can interact directly with the Python interpreter by entering statements at the prompt.

Menu Bar

Version Banner

Interactive
Prompt

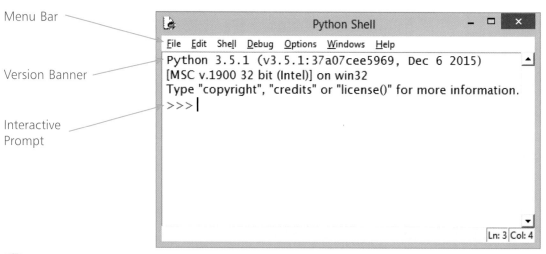

Hot tip

Most programming languages require text strings to be enclosed in quote marks to differentiate them from program code. By convention, Python coders use single quotes.

If the interpreter understands your entry it will respond with an appropriate reply, otherwise it will report an error.

You can make the interpreter print out a string of text by entering a Python **print()** function statement that encloses your string within quote marks inside the parentheses at the interactive prompt.

You can also make the interpreter print out the result of a simple arithmetic sum by entering a valid sum statement at the prompt.

If your statement is not valid, such as a sum that attempts to divide a number by zero, the interpreter will print out an error message helpfully describing the nature of the error.

...cont'd

1 Open an IDLE Shell Window then precisely enter this statement at the interactive prompt
print('Hello World!' **)**

2 Next, hit the Return key to see the interpreter's response

```
Python Shell                          _ ☐ ✕
File  Edit  Shell  Debug  Options  Windows  Help
>>> print( 'Hello World!' )
Hello World!
>>>
```

Hot tip

Spaces in statements are ignored – so **8+4** can be entered without spaces.

3 Now, enter this sum statement at the interactive prompt
8 + 4

4 Hit Return to see the interpreter print the result total

```
Python Shell                          _ ☐ ✕
File  Edit  Shell  Debug  Options  Windows  Help
>>> 8 + 4
12
>>>
```

13

5 Enter this invalid statement at the interactive prompt
8 / 0

6 Hit Return to see the interpreter print an error message

Don't forget

The Shell Window is mostly used to test snippets of code.

```
Python Shell                          _ ☐ ✕
File  Edit  Shell  Debug  Options  Windows  Help
>>> 8 / 0
Traceback (most recent call last):
  File "<pyshell#2>", line 1, in <module>
    8 / 0
ZeroDivisionError: division by zero
>>>
```

Getting help

The IDLE Shell Window provides a great Help utility where you can find help on any Python topic when coding Python programs. Help can be sought by entering a Python **help()** statement at the interactive **>>>** prompt. A welcome message appears and the prompt changes to **help>** to denote you are now in Help mode.

 Open an IDLE Shell Window then precisely enter this statement at the interactive prompt
help( )

 Next, hit the Return key to enter Help mode

Hot tip

The Help utility welcome message also contains handy hints – but are omitted here for brevity.

```
                        Python Shell              –  □  ×
File  Edit  Shell  Debug  Options  Windows  Help
>>> help()

Welcome to Python 3.5's help utility!

help>|
```

 Now, enter this topic name at the Help utility prompt
keywords

 Hit Return to list all keywords of the Python language

Don't forget

Keywords are the vocabulary of a programming language. Note that Python keywords are case-sensitive – these are all in lowercase except **False**, **None**, and **True**.

```
                        Python Shell              –  □  ×
File  Edit  Shell  Debug  Options  Windows  Help
help> keywords

Here is a list of the Python keywords.
Enter any keyword to get more help.

False        def         if          raise
None         del         import       return
True         elif        in          try
and          else        is          while
as           except      lambda       with
assert       finally     nonlocal     yield
break        for         not
class        from        or
continue     global       pass

help>|
```

...cont'd

5 Then, enter this command at the Help utility prompt
quit

6 Hit Return to exit Help and return to an interactive Shell Window prompt

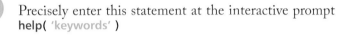

```
Python Shell                       – ☐  ✕

File  Edit  Shell  Debug  Options  Windows  Help

help> quit

You are now leaving help and returning to the Python interpreter.
If you want to ask for help on a particular object directly from the
interpreter, you can type "help(object)".  Executing "help('string')"
has the same effect as typing a particular string at the help> prompt.
>>> |
```

There are no parentheses required after the **quit** instruction – here it is a Help utility command, not a Python statement.

When you just want help on a single topic you can simply enter the topic name within quote marks inside the parentheses of a **help()** statement at the interactive prompt:

7 Precisely enter this statement at the interactive prompt
help('keywords' **)**

8 Hit Return to list all keywords of the Python language and remain at an interactive Shell Window prompt

```
Python Shell                       – ☐  ✕

File  Edit  Shell  Debug  Options  Windows  Help

>>> help('keywords')

Here is a list of the Python keywords.
Enter any keyword to get more help.

False          def          if           raise
None           del          import           return
True           elif         in           try
and            else         is           while
as             except         lambda         with
assert         finally        nonlocal       yield
break          for          not
class          from         or
continue         global         pass

>>> |
```

Keywords have special meaning in a programming language – they cannot be used to name items in your code.

Saving programs

The IDLE Shell Window, described on the previous page, is a great place to try out snippets of code, but cannot save your code. Happily IDLE also provides an Edit Window where you can create longer pieces of programming code that can be stored in a (.py) file on your computer. This means you can easily re-run the code without re-typing all the instructions at the Shell Window >>> prompt and this lets you edit your code to try new ideas. The procedure to create, save, and run your code looks like this:

The procedure described here will be used to demonstrate the code examples given throughout this book.

Hot tip

- Open an Edit Window from the Shell Window by selecting File, New File from the Shell Window menu items – or by pressing the Ctrl + N shortcut keys

- Type code into the Edit Window then save it by selecting File, Save from the Edit Window menu items – or by pressing the Ctrl + S shortcut keys

- Run saved code from the Edit Window by selecting Run, Run Module from the Edit Window menu items – or by pressing the F5 shortcut key

Output from your program code will appear in the Shell Window as the program runs, or a helpful error message will appear there if the interpreter discovers an error in your code.

1   Open an IDLE Shell Window then select the File, New File menu item to open an IDLE Edit Window

Hot tip

Notice the File, Open and File, Recent Files menu items that can be used to re-run program code previously saved.

Python Shell	— □ ✕

File   Edit   Shell   Debug   Options   Windows   Help

New File	Ctrl+N
Open...	Ctrl+O
Recent Files	▶
Open Module...	Alt+M
Class Browser	Alt+C
Path Browser	
Save	Ctrl+S
Save As...	Ctrl+Shift+S
Save Copy As...	Alt+Shift+S
Print Window	Ctrl+P
Close	Alt+F4
Exit	Ctrl+Q

16

2 Now, in the IDLE Edit Window, precisely enter this code
print('Hello World!' **)**

```
*Untitled*                                    –  □  ×
File  Edit  Format  Run  Options  Windows  Help
print( 'Hello World!' )                                ▲
```

helloworld.py

3 Next, in the IDLE Edit Window, select the File, Save menu items, to open the Save As dialog, then save your program code as a file named **helloworld.py**

```
Save As                                       ×
Save in:   MyCode              ▼  ← ⬆ ➡* ▦▼

            helloworld.py
Recent places   PY File
            25 bytes

File name:    helloworld.py          ▼      Save
Save as type: Python files (*.py,*.pyw) ▼    Cancel
```

Hot tip

Your program code
can be saved at any
convenient location on
your computer – here it
is saved in a directory
created at **C:\MyCode**
that will be used for all
examples in this book.

17

4 Finally, in the IDLE Edit Window, select the Run, Run Module menu items, to run your program code and see the output appear in the Shell Window

```
helloworld.py - C:\MyCode\helloworld.py  –  □  ×
File  Edit  Format  Run  Options  Windows  Help
print( 'Hello Wo                                   ▲
            Python Shell
            Check Module  Alt+X
            Run Module    F5
```

```
Python Shell                            –  □  ×
File  Edit  Shell  Debug  Options  Windows  Help
>>> ============= RESTART ================  ▲
>>>
Hello World!
>>> |
```

Hot tip

Notice that the Shell
Window restarts
whenever it runs your
program code afresh.

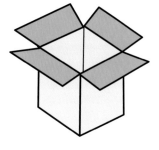

Storing values

One essential feature of all computer programming languages is the ability to store data values in the program code. This ability is provided by a simple data structure called a "variable". A variable is a container in which an item of data can be stored, much like a real-life object can be stored in a box.

When creating a variable you give it a name of your choice, subject to the naming conventions of the programming language, that acts like a label on a box. The data item stored within the variable can subsequently be retrieved using its given name – just as you can find a real-life object in a box by reading its label.

Data to be stored in a variable is assigned in a Python program declaration statement with the = assignment operator. For example, to store the numeric value eight in a variable named "a":

`a = 8`

The stored value can then be retrieved using the variable's name, so that the statement **print(a)** will output the stored value **8**. That variable can subsequently be assigned a different value, so its value can vary as the program proceeds – hence the term "variable".

In Python programming a variable must be assigned an initial value ("initialized") in the statement that declares it in a program – otherwise the interpreter will report a "not defined" error.

Multiple variables can be initialized with a common value in a single statement using a sequence of = assignments. For example, to initialize variables named "a", "b" and "c" each with a numeric value of eight like this:

`a = b = c = 8`

Some programming languages, such as Java, demand you specify in its declaration what type of data a variable may contain. This reserves a specific amount of memory space and is known as "static typing". Python variables, on the other hand, have no such limitation and adjust the memory allocation to suit the various data values assigned to their variables ("dynamic typing"). This means they can store integer whole numbers, floating-point numbers, text strings, or Boolean values of **True** or **False** as required.

Hot tip

Programming languages that require variable types to be specified are alternatively known as "strongly typed", whereas those that do not are alternatively known as "loosely typed".

① Open an IDLE Edit Window then enter code to create a variable named "var" to store a whole number integer
```
var = 8
```

② Next, add a statement to display the stored integer value
```
print( var )
```

firstvar.py

③ Assign a new floating-point number to the variable then add a statement to display the stored float value
```
var = 3.142
print( var )
```

④ Now, assign a text string to the variable then add a statement to display the stored string value
```
var = 'Coding for Beginners in easy steps'
print( var )
```

⑤ Finally, assign a logical truth value to the variable then add a statement to display the stored Boolean value
```
var = True
print( var )
```

⑥ Save the file (File, Save) then run the program (Run, Run Module) to see the stored values displayed in output

```
Python Shell                               –  □  ✕
File  Edit  Shell  Debug  Options  Windows  Help
>>> ============= RESTART ============== ===
>>>
8
3.142
Coding for Beginners in easy steps
True
>>> |
```

Don't forget

Text string data must be enclosed within quote marks to denote the start and end of that particular string.

Adding comments

When you begin to code longer programs it is useful to add comments at the start of each piece of code describing the purpose of that piece. This makes the code more easily understood by others, and by yourself when revisiting the code at a later date. In the Python programming language everything on a single line after a **#** hash character is ignored by the interpreter. This means that a single-line comment can be inserted after a **#** character.

comment.py

1 Open an IDLE Edit Window then enter commented code to initialize a variable and display its status

```
# Initialize program status
running = True
print( 'Run state: ' , running )
```

2 Save the file then run the program to see the comment get ignored and the stored value displayed in output

```
>>> ============= RESTART =============
>>>
Run state: True
>>>
```

To readily identify aspects of your code, IDLE automatically colorizes your code, both in the Shell Window and the Edit Window, with the default colors listed in the table below:

Don't forget

Code listed in the steps throughout this book also use the default IDLE colors for consistency.

Color:	Description:	Example:
	Built-in function names	**print()**
	Strings in quote marks	'Hello World!'
	Symbols, numbers and names	**8 + 4**
	Shell Window output Coder-created function names	**Hello World! my_function()**
	Keywords	True
	Edit Window comments and Shell Window errors	# My comments ZeroDivisionError

Naming rules

Keywords:		
False	None	True
and	as	assert
break	class	continue
def	del	elif
else	except	finally
for	from	global
if	import	in
is	lambda	nonlocal
not	or	pass
raise	return	try
while	with	yield

Hot tip

It is good programming practice to choose meaningful names that reflect the nature of the variable's content.

Variable containers that you create in your code to store data within a program can be given any name of your choosing – providing you do not use any of the programming language keywords, such as the Python keywords in the table above, and the name adheres to the naming rules listed in the table below:

Naming rule:	Example:
CANNOT contain any keywords	True
CANNOT contain arithmetic operators	a+b*c
CANNOT contain symbols	%$#@!
CANNOT contain any spaces	no spaces
CANNOT start with a number	2bad
CAN contain numbers elsewhere	good1
CAN contain letters of mixed case	UPdown
CAN contain underscores	is_ok

Beware

Variable names are case-sensitive in Python – so variables named "VAR", "Var", and "var" would be treated as three separate variables.

Summary

- A computer program is a set of instructions, written by a coder, that enable computers to become useful

- The electronic components of a computer are its hardware, whereas program instructions are its software

- Computers understand low-level machine code

- High-level programming languages in human-readable form get automatically translated into low-level machine code

- Programming languages possess data structures to store information and control structures to determine progress

- The Python programming language has simple syntax, requires no compilation, and includes a library of functions

- Python's development environment is called IDLE

- IDLE provides a Shell Window containing an interactive prompt for testing and an Edit Window for coding programs

- The IDLE Help utility is accessed by entering a **help()** statement at a Shell Window prompt

- After typing program code into an IDLE Edit Window it must first be saved as a file before the program can be run

- Output from a program run from the Edit Window appears in the Shell Window, or a helpful error message appears there

- A variable data structure is a named container that allows a single item of data to be stored for use by a program

- Data stored in a variable can be retrieved using that variable's name and may be replaced by assigning a new value

- Variables in Python programming can store any type of data

- Comment lines can usefully be added to program code after beginning the line with a **#** hash character

- Variable names must not use any of the programming language keywords and must adhere to its naming rules

2 Saving data

This chapter demonstrates how to create code to use various types of data stored inside your programs.

Storing input

The ability to store and replace coded program data in a variable is great, but this ability can also be used to store data input by a user – allowing your programs to become interactive.

In Python programming a built-in **input()** function can be used to accept user input from a keyboard and assign it to a variable. Optionally, this function can specify a string, within quote marks inside its parentheses, that will be displayed to request the input. The program will wait until the user hits the Return key before assigning their input to the variable and proceeding onwards.

Stored variable values can be output by the built-in **print()** function by specifying the variable name within the function's parentheses. Multiple values may also be specified for output as a comma-separated list within the parentheses.

input.py

 Open an IDLE Edit Window then enter this code to request user input with which to initialize a variable
name = input('Please enter your name: ' **)**

 Next, add a statement to output both a string and the value stored within the variable
print('Hello' **, name)**

 Now, add statements to output a string then both a string and the value stored within the variable once more
print('Welcome to Coding for Beginners' **)**
print('Remember to have fun' **, name , '!')**

Don't forget

There is no need to include spaces in the comma-separated lists – they are ignored by the interpreter but are shown here for clarity.

Save then run the program, enter your name when requested, and hit Return to see your name in the output

```
Python Shell                    – □ ✕

File  Edit  Shell  Debug  Options  Windows  Help

>>> ============= RESTART ==============
>>>
Please enter your name: Mike
Hello Mike
Welcome to Coding for Beginners
Remember to have fun Mike !
>>>
```

Controlling output

As the example on the facing page demonstrates, a value stored in a variable remains available for repeated use until it is replaced by a new value or until the program ends.

There are also two points worth noting with regard to this example's output. Firstly, the **print()** function automatically adds an invisible **\n** newline character after its output – so the next **print()** function output will by default appear on the next line below. Secondly, the **print()** function automatically adds a space between each item when a comma-separated list is specified for output.

You can override the automatic newline behavior by specifying that the line should end with a space, rather than the **\n** default. You can also avoid the automatic spacing behavior by "concatenating" items with a **+** symbol, rather than a comma.

 1 Open an IDLE Edit Window then enter this code to request user input with which to initialize a variable
name = input('Please enter your name: ' **)**

2 Next, add a statement to output a string and the value stored within the variable – but without a final newline
print('Hello ' **+ name , end =** ' ' **)**

3 Now, add statements to output a string then a string concatenated to the value stored within the variable
print('- Welcome to Coding for Beginners' **)**
print('Remember to have fun ' **+ name +** '!' **)**

4 Save then run the program, enter your name when requested, and hit Return to see controlled output

concat.py

Hot tip

Notice that the strings have been edited to nicely format the output.

```
                Python Shell            – □ ×
 File  Edit  Shell  Debug  Options  Windows  Help
>>> ============= RESTART ==============
>>>
Please enter your name: Sandra
Hello Sandra – Welcome to Coding for Beginners
Remember to have fun Sandra!
>>> |
```

Recognizing types

There are four essential types of data you can represent when coding a computer program and that can be stored in variables. Although variables in the Python language can store any type of data it is important to understand the different types as you will sometimes need to convert from one type to another in your code:

Data type:	Description:		Example:
str	A string of characters, which can include letters, numbers, spaces, and symbols		'Daytona 500'
int	An integer whole number, which DOES NOT have a decimal point part		1000
float	A floating-point number, which DOES have a decimal point part		98.6
bool	A Boolean logical truth value, which is either True or False		True

Strings are simply any collection of characters you can enter from the computer keyboard, grouped together within quote marks. Variables recognize a value being assigned to it as belonging to the **str** "class" if that value is enclosed within quote marks.

Numbers are any numeric value you can enter from the keyboard but are defined by the inclusion or omission of a decimal point. Variables recognize a numeric value being assigned to it as belonging to the **int** "class" if that value has no decimal point or as belonging to the **float** class if it does indeed have a decimal point.

Booleans are a logical truth value. Variables recognize a Boolean value being assigned to it as belonging to the **bool** "class" by the keywords **True** and **False**, or if that value evaluates to True or False.

In Python programming you can easily discover the type of data stored within a variable by specifying that variable's name within the parentheses of the built-in **type()** function.

Beware

Integer **int** numbers should not include any punctuation – so code one thousand as 1000 rather than 1,000.

Don't forget

String **str** values must always be enclosed with quote marks.

1 Open an IDLE Edit Window and initialize a variable by assigning it a string, then display its value and data type
```
race = 'Daytona 500'
print( race , 'is' , type( race ) )
```

types.py

2 Next, initialize a variable by assigning it a whole number then display its value and data type
```
kilo = 1000
print( kilo , 'is' , type( kilo ) )
```

3 Now, initialize a variable by assigning it a decimal number, then display its value and data type
```
temp = 98.6
print( temp , 'is' , type( temp ) )
```

4 Initialize a variable by assigning it a truth keyword then display its value and data type
```
flag = True
print( flag , 'is' , type( flag ) )
```

5 Finally, replace the last variable value with a truth result of a comparison, then again display its value and data type
```
flag = 4 > 8
print( flag , 'is' , type( flag ) )
```

6 Save then run the program to discover the types of data stored within the variables you have created

```
                    Python Shell           –  ☐  ✕
File  Edit  Shell  Debug  Options  Windows  Help
>>> ============== RESTART ===============
>>>
Daytona 500 is <class 'str'>
1000 is <class 'int'>
98.6 is <class 'float'>
True is <class 'bool'>
False is <class 'bool'>
>>>|
```

Hot tip

The comparison here examines whether 4 is greater than 8, which is of course untrue. Comparisons are demonstrated fully in the next chapter.

Converting data

Often you will need to convert data in your programs to perform some kind of manipulation – such as arithmetic or concatenation. Arithmetic can only be performed on numeric data types, such as **int** and **float** data, whereas concatenation can only be performed on string data types, such as **str** data.

Python provides several built-in functions that allow you to easily convert data in your programs to a different data type. These do not convert the original specified value itself but merely return a converted representation of its value. In programming terms this is known as a "cast" operation:

Numeric values in your code should not be enclosed within quote marks – numbers within quotes will be seen as string values!

Function:	Description:
int(x)	Converts *x* to an integer whole number
float(x)	Converts *x* to a decimal floating-point number
str(x)	Converts *x* to a string representation

Numeric values assigned to variables manually in your code are automatically appointed the appropriate data type of **int** or **float**. Values assigned to variables from users by the built-in **input()** function are, however, always automatically appointed the **str** string data type – even when they are simply numeric values! This means they must be converted (cast) to an appropriate numeric type of **int** or **float** before you can perform arithmetic with them.

Conversely numeric values assigned to variables manually in your code, which are automatically appointed the appropriate data type of **int** or **float**, cannot be concatenated into a string. This means they must be converted to a **str** data type for inclusion in a string.

Arithmetic performed on an **int** and **float** data type together will be automatically cast into a **float** result. Cast values to the **float** data type to allow for decimal number input.

In Python, as in many other programming languages, the + symbol has more than one purpose according to its context. Where the + symbol is used between two numeric values it performs an addition (seen as an "addition operator") but where the + symbol is used between two string values it performs a concatenation (seen as a "concatenation operator"). Variables that are assigned the result of either kind of operation will automatically be appointed the appropriate data type of the result.

...cont'd

1 Open an IDLE Edit Window and initialize two variables by assigning them numeric user input
```
num1 = input( 'Please enter a whole number: ' )
num2 = input( 'Now enter another whole number: ' )
```

cast.py

2 Next, display the data type of each variable to see the numeric values are, in fact, stored as strings
```
print( 'Input is: ' , type( num1 ) , type( num2 ) )
```

3 Now, use the + operator to attempt addition, but see the result gets concatenated as a **str** data type
```
total = num1 + num2
print( 'Total:' , total , type( total ) )
```

4 Again, use the + operator to attempt addition, but cast the stored values to see the result as an **int** data type
```
total = int( num1 ) + int( num2 )
print( 'Total:' , total , type( total ) )
```

5 Finally, cast the stored values as a **float** data type and concatenate the **float** result value to the output **str** string
```
total = float( num1 ) + float( num2 )
print( 'Total:' , str( total ) , type( total ) )
```

29

6 Save then run the program to see the stored data types converted by casting them with the built-in functions

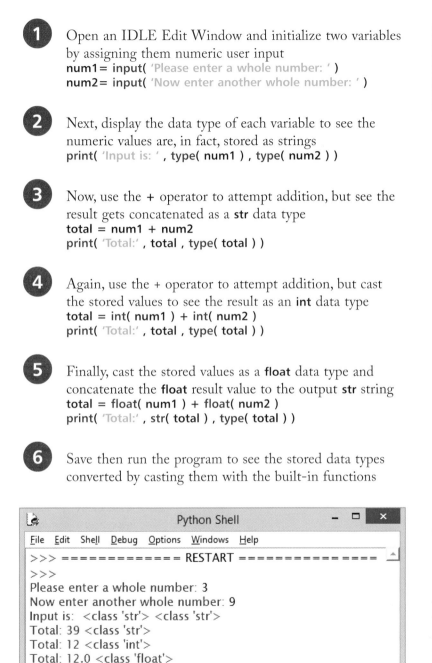

```
Python Shell                                  –  □  ×
File  Edit  Shell  Debug  Options  Windows  Help
>>> ============= RESTART ================
>>>
Please enter a whole number: 3
Now enter another whole number: 9
Input is:  <class 'str'> <class 'str'>
Total: 39 <class 'str'>
Total: 12 <class 'int'>
Total: 12.0 <class 'float'>
>>>
```

Beware

If you forget to convert to the correct data type the interpreter will report an error – try adding an **int** to a **str** data type to see the error message.

Guessing game

The previous simple examples have illustrated how variables can be used to store text string values, numeric integer and floating-point decimal values, and Boolean truth values in your programs. Now, they can be used to create a Guessing Game program by storing a random generated integer whose value the user will have to guess, a Boolean truth value that will end the game when the user guesses correctly, and a string containing the user's guess.

The code in this example includes some features that are only demonstrated later in this book, but as Python is an easily human-readable programming language you should be able to understand in principle how this program works.

guess.py

 Open an IDLE Edit Window and begin a program by importing a "random" library class that provides random number generator functions

```
import random
```

 Now, initialize three variables – a generated random number between one and 20, a Boolean value that will remain True as long as the game is in progress, and a zero value that will later store a number input by the user

```
num = random.randint( 1 , 20 )
flag = True
guess = 0
```

3 Next, display a message asking the user to make a guess

```
print( 'Guess my number 1-20 : ' , end = ' ' )
```

4 Then, precisely copy this code that will compare the stored user's guess to the stored random number

```
while flag == True :

    guess = input( )
    if not guess.isdigit() :
        print( 'Invalid! Enter only digits 1-20' )
        break
    elif int( guess ) < num :
        print( 'Too low, try again : ' , end = ' ' )
    elif int( guess ) > num :
        print( 'Too high,try again : ' , end = ' ' )
    else :
        print( 'Correct... My number is ' + guess )
        flag = False
```

Beware

Many program languages use characters such as { } to group statements together but Python uses indentation – so the indentation shown here must be correctly preserved.

5 Save then run the program and enter guesses to see your input compared to a stored random number

```
Python Shell                          −  □  ✕

File  Edit  Shell  Debug  Options  Windows  Help

>>> ============= RESTART =============
>>>
Guess My Number 1–20 : ten
Invalid! Enter only digits 1–20
>>> ============= RESTART =============
>>>
Guess My Number 1–20 : 10.0
Invalid! Enter only digits 1–20
>>> ============= RESTART =============
>>>
Guess My Number 1–20 : 10
Too high,try again : 2
Too low, try again : 7
Too high,try again : 4
Correct... My number is 4
>>> |
```

Notice that the program rejects user input of **str** string or **float** values.

Guessing Game in Python – program analysis

● The **random** library class's **randint()** function specifies an upper and lower random range within its parentheses

● The **flag** variable specifies an initial program condition that will allow the program to start examining the user's input

● The **while** keyword specifies a "loop" control structure that will repeat the statements it contains until a tested condition fails

● The **if not guess.isdigit()** test specifies an action to **break** the loop if the user input is not an integer whole number

● The **elif int(guess) < num** test specifies an alternative action if the cast user input is lower than the stored random number

● The **elif int(guess) > num** test specifies an alternative action if the cast user input is higher than the stored random number

● The **else** keyword specifies a final alternative action to change the program condition, thereby ending the program

You need not yet understand this program in detail – each aspect is explained by examples later in this book.

Correcting errors

When coding programs there are three common types of error that can occur. It is useful to recognize these different error types in Python programming so they can be corrected more easily:

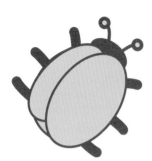

- **Syntax Error** – occurs when the interpreter encounters code that does not conform to the Python language rules. For example, a missing quote mark around a string. The interpreter halts and reports the error without executing the program.

- **Runtime Error** – occurs during execution of the program, at the time when the program runs. For example, when a variable name is later mis-typed so the variable cannot be recognized. The interpreter runs the program but halts at the error and reports the nature of the error as an "Exception".

- **Semantic Error** – occurs when the program performs unexpectedly. For example, when order precedence has not been specified in an expression. The interpreter runs the program and does not report an error.

Programming errors are often called "bugs" and the process of tracking them down is often called "debugging".

Correcting syntax and runtime errors is fairly straightforward, as the interpreter reports where the error occurred or the nature of the error type, but semantic errors require code examination.

 Open an IDLE Edit Window then add a statement to output a string that omits a closing quote mark
print('Coding for Beginners in easy steps **)**

 Save then run the program to see the interpreter highlight the syntax error and indicate its nature

syntax.py

Beware

The red syntax error indicator points to the line where the End Of Line (EOL) error occurs.

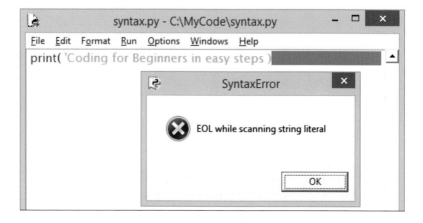

3 Insert a quote mark before the closing parenthesis to terminate the string and save then run the program again – to see the error has been corrected

4 Next, begin a new program by initializing a variable then try to output its value with an incorrect variable name – to see the interpreter report a runtime error

```
title = 'Coding for Beginners in easy steps'
print( titel )
```

runtime.py

```
Python Shell                                    −  □  ×
File  Edit  Shell  Debug  Options  Windows  Help
>>> ============= RESTART ===============
>>>
Traceback (most recent call last):
  File "C:/MyCode/runtime.py", line 2, in <module>
    print( titel )
NameError: name 'titel' is not defined
>>>|
```

Hot tip

Details of how to handle runtime Exception errors in your script code are provided on page 70.

5 Amend the variable name to match that in the variable declaration and save then run the program again – to see the error has been corrected

6 Now, begin a new program by initializing a variable then try to output an expression using its value without explicit precedence – to see a possibly unexpected result of 28

```
num = 3
print( 'Result: ' , num * 8 + 4 )
```

semantic.py

```
Python Shell                                    −  □  ×
File  Edit  Shell  Debug  Options  Windows  Help
>>> ============= RESTART ===============
>>>
Result: 28
>>>|
```

7 Add parentheses to group the expression as **3 * (8 + 4)** then save the file and run the program again – to see the expected result of 36, correcting the semantic error

33

Summary

- Variables can be used to store data values specified in program code and to store data values input by a user

- A value stored in a variable remains available for repeated use until it is replaced by a new value or until the program ends

- The Python built-in **input()** function can assign input to a variable and may optionally specify a string to be displayed

- The Python built-in **print()** function can specify multiple values for output as a comma-separated list in its parentheses

- By default, the **print()** function will automatically add a **\n** newline after its output unless an **end** alternative is specified

- The **+** concatenation operator can join two strings together

- Data types are essentially **str** text strings, **int** integer numbers, **float** decimal numbers, or **bool** Boolean truth values

- Booleans are logical truth values that are represented in Python by the **True** and **False** keywords

- The Python built-in **type()** function can identify to which class data type a value in any specified variable belongs

- Values assigned to a variable by the Python built-in **input()** function are always appointed the **str** string data type

- Data types can be converted for manipulation using the Python built-in **int()**, **float()**, and **str()** casting functions

- Arithmetic performed on an **int** integer number and a **float** decimal number will produce a **float** data type result

- Syntax errors due to incorrect code are recognized by the interpreter before execution of the program

- Runtime errors due to exceptions are recognized by the interpreter during execution of the program

- Semantic errors due to unexpected performance are not recognized by the interpreter

3 Performing operations

This chapter demonstrates how to use operator symbols in your code statements.

Doing arithmetic

The arithmetical "operators" commonly used in coding computer programs use a + symbol for addition and a - symbol for subtraction, as you would expect. Typically, they also use an * asterisk for multiplication, rather than an **x** symbol, and a / forward slash for division, rather than a ÷ symbol.

The arithmetical operators used to code Python programs are listed in the table below, together with the operation they perform:

Operator:	Operation:
+	Addition
-	Subtraction
*	Multiplication
/	Division
%	Remainder
//	Floor division
**	Exponent

The + operator adds two numbers together and the - operator subtracts the second number from the first number.

The * operator multiplies the first number by the second number and the / operator divides the first number by the second number.

The % remainder operator divides the first number by the second number and returns the remainder of the operation. This is useful to determine if a number has an odd or even value.

The // floor division operator performs just like the / division operator but truncates the result at the decimal point – removing any floating point part from the resulting number.

The ** exponent operator returns the result of the first number raised to the power of the second number.

Hot tip

Values used with operators to form expressions are called "operands" – in the expression **2 + 3** the numerical values **2** and **3** are the operands.

1 Start a new program by creating two variables containing whole numbers (integers)
```
a = 8
b = 2
```

2 Next, display the result of adding the numbers
```
print( 'Addition: \t' , a , '+' , b , '=' , a + b )
```

arithmetic.py

3 Now, display the result of subtracting the numbers
```
print( 'Subtraction:\t' , a , '-' , b , '=' , a - b )
```

4 Then, display the result of multiplying the numbers
```
print( 'Multiplication:\t' , a , 'x' , b , '=' , a * b )
```

5 Display the result of dividing the numbers, both with and without the floating-point part
```
print( 'Division:  \t' , a , '÷' , b , '=' , a / b )
print( 'Floor Division:\t' , a , '÷' , b , '=' , a // b )
```

Beware

Here, the special \t character sequence adds an invisible tab character to format the output.

6 Next, display the remainder after dividing the numbers
```
print( 'Remainder:\t' , a , '%' , b , '=' , a % b )
```

37

7 Finally, display the result of raising the first number to the power of the second number
```
print( 'Exponent:\t ' , a , '² = ' , a ** b , sep = '' )
```

8 Save then run the program to see the result of the arithmetical operations

```
                  Python Shell              -  □  ×
File  Edit  Shell  Debug  Options  Windows  Help
>>> ============= RESTART ================
>>>
Addition:          8 + 2 = 10
Subtraction:       8 - 2 = 6
Multiplication:    8 x 2 = 16
Division:          8 ÷ 2 = 4.0
Floor Division:    8 ÷ 2 = 4
Remainder          8 % 2 = 0
Exponent:          8² = 64
>>>|
```

Don't forget

You can use the **sep** parameter to explicitly specify the separation between output – here, it specifies no spaces by assigning two unspaced single quote marks.

Assigning values

The assignment operator commonly used in coding computer programs simply uses a = symbol to assign a value to a variable. Optionally, this may be combined with an arithmetical operator to perform arithmetic and assignment in one single operation.

The assignment operators used to code Python programs are listed in the table below together with the operation they perform:

Operator:	Example:	Equivalent:
=	a = b	a = b
+=	a += b	a = (a + b)
-=	a -= b	a = (a - b)
*=	a *= b	a = (a * b)
/=	a /= b	a = (a / b)
%=	a %= b	a = (a % b)
//=	a //= b	a = (a // b)
**=	a **= b	a = (a ** b)

In the example above, variable **a** is assigned the value contained in variable **b** – so that becomes the new value in the **a** variable.

The += operator is useful to add a value onto an existing value stored in the **a** variable – making it a combined total value.

In the example above the += operator first adds the value contained in variable **a** to the value contained in variable **b**. It then assigns the result to become the new value stored in variable **a**.

All these other operators work in the same way by making the arithmetical operation between the two values first, then assigning the result of that operation to the first variable – to become its new stored value.

With the %= operator the first operand **a** is divided by the second operand **b** then the remainder is assigned to the **a** variable.

Don't forget

It is important to regard the = operator to mean "assign" rather than "equals" to avoid confusion with the == equality operator.

1 Start a new program by creating two variables containing integer numbers and displays both assigned values

```
a = 8
b = 4
print( 'Assign Values:\t' , 'a =' , a , '\tb =' , b )
```

assign.py

2 Next, add and assign a new value to the first variable and display its stored value

```
a += b
print( 'Add & Assign:\t' ,'a =' , a , '\t(8 += 4)' )
```

3 Now, subtract and assign a new value to the first variable and display its stored value, then multiply and assign a value to the first variable and display its stored value

```
a -= b
print( 'Subtract & Assign:\t' , 'a =' , a , '\t(12 - 4)' )
a *= b
print( 'Multiply & Assign:\t' , 'a =' , a , '\t(8 x 4)' )
```

4 Finally, divide and assign a new value to the first variable and display its stored value, then remainder and assign a value to the first variable and display its stored value

```
a /= b
print( 'Divide & Assign:\t' , 'a =' , a , '\t(32 ÷ 4)' )
a %= b
print( 'Remainder & Assign:\t' , 'a =' , a , '\t(8 % 4)' )
```

5 Save then run the program to see the result of the assignment operations

```
┌─────────────────────────────────────────────────┐
│ 🖳            Python Shell          – □ ✕        │
├─────────────────────────────────────────────────┤
│ File  Edit  Shell  Debug  Options  Windows  Help │
├─────────────────────────────────────────────────┤
│ >>> ============= RESTART ============ ====  ▲  │
│ >>>                                             │
│ Hello World!                                    │
│ >>>                                             │
│ Assign Values:      a = 8     b = 4             │
│ Add & Assign:       a = 12    (8 += 4)          │
│ Subtract & Assign:  a = 8     (12 – 4)          │
│ Multiply & Assign:  a = 32    (8 x 4)           │
│ Divide & Assign:    a = 8.0   (32 ÷ 4)          │
│ Modulus & Assign:   a = 0.0   (8 % 4)           │
│ >>> |                                           │
└─────────────────────────────────────────────────┘
```

Beware

Unlike the = assign operator, the == equality operator compares operands and is described on page 40.

Comparing values

The operators that are commonly used in Python programming to compare two operand values are listed in the table below:

Operator:	Comparative test:
==	Equality
!=	Inequality
>	Greater than
<	Less than
>=	Greater than or equal to
<=	Less than or equal to

The == equality operator compares two operands and will return **True** if both are equal in value, otherwise it will return a **False** value. If both are the same number they are equal, or if both are characters their ASCII code values are compared numerically to achieve the comparison result.

Conversely, the != inequality operator returns **True** if two operands are not equal, using the same rules as the == equality operator, otherwise it returns **False**. Equality and inequality operators are useful in testing the state of two variables to perform conditional branching in a program according to the result.

The > "greater than" operator compares two operands and will return **True** if the first is greater in value than the second, or it will return **False** if it is equal or less in value. The < "less than" operator makes the same comparison but returns **True** if the first operand is less in value than the second, otherwise it returns **False**. A > "greater than" or < "less than" operator is often used to test the value of an iteration counter in a loop.

Adding the = operator after a > "greater than" or < "less than" operator makes it also return **True** if the two operands are exactly equal in value.

Hot tip

A-Z uppercase characters have ASCII code values 65-90 and a-z lowercase characters have ASCII code values 97-122.

1 Start a new program by initializing five variables with values for comparison
```
nil = 0
num = 0
top = 1
cap = 'A'
low = 'a'
```

comparison.py

2 Next, add statements to display the results of numeric and character equality comparisons
```
print( 'Equality : \t' , nil , '==' , num , nil == num )
print( 'Equality : \t' , cap , '==' , low , cap == low )
```

3 Now, add a statement to display the result of an inequality comparison
```
print( 'Inequality :\t' , nil , '!=' , top , nil != top )
```

4 Then, add statements to display the results of greater and lesser comparisons
```
print( 'Greater : \t' , nil , '>' , top , nil > top )
print( 'Lesser :   \t' , nil , '<' , top , nil < top )
```

The \t escape sequence shown here adds an invisible tab character to format the output.

5 Finally, add statements to display the results of greater or equal and lesser or equal comparisons
```
print( 'More Or Equal :\t' , nil , '>=' , num , nil >= num )
print( 'Less or Equal :\t' , top , '<=' , num , top <= num )
```

6 Save then run the program – to see the result of comparison operations

```
Python Shell                          –  □  ✕

File  Edit  Shell  Debug  Options  Windows  Help

>>> ============== RESTART ===============
>>>
Equality :          0 == 0 True
Equality :          A == a False
Inequality :        0 != 1 True
Greater :           0 > 1 False
Lesser :            0 < 1 True
More Or Equal :     0 >= 0 True
Less or Equal :     1 <= 0 False
>>>
```

The ASCII code value for uppercase "A" is 65 but for lowercase "a" it's 97 – so their comparison here returns **False**.

Finding truth

The logical operators most commonly used in Python programming are listed in the table below:

Operator:	Operation:
and	Logical AND
or	Logical OR
not	Logical NOT

The logical operators are used with operands that have Boolean values of **True** or **False**, or are values that convert to **True** or **False**.

The (logical AND) **and** operator will evaluate two operands and return **True** only if both operands themselves are **True**. Otherwise the **and** operator will return **False**. This is useful in programming to perform "conditional branching" where the direction of a program is determined by testing two conditions – if both conditions are satisfied, the program will go in a certain direction, otherwise it will take a different direction.

Unlike the **and** operator that needs both operands to be **True**, the (logical OR) **or** operator will evaluate its two operands and return **True** if either one of the operands itself returns **True**. If neither operand returns **True**, then the **or** operator will return **False**. This is useful in programming to perform a certain action if either one of two test conditions has been met.

The (logical NOT) **not** operator is a unary operator that is used before a single operand. It returns the inverse value of the given operand, so if the variable **a** had a value of **True** then **not a** would have a value of **False**. The **not** operator is useful in programming to toggle the value of a variable in successive loop iterations with a statement like **a = not a**. This ensures that on each iteration of the loop the Boolean value is reversed, like flicking a light switch on and off.

Hot tip

The term "Boolean" refers to a system of logical thought developed by the English mathematician George Boole (1815-1864).

...cont'd

1 Start a new program by initializing two variables with Boolean values for logical evaluation

```
a = True
b = False
```

logic.py

2 Add statements to display the results of AND evaluations

```
print( 'AND Logic:' )
print( 'a and a =' , a and a )
print( 'a and b =' , a and b )
print( 'b and b =' , b and b )
```

3 Add statements to display the results of OR evaluations

```
print( '\nOR Logic:' )
print( 'a or a =' , a or a )
print( 'a or b =' , a or b )
print( 'b or b =' , b or b )
```

Hot tip

In Python programming, Boolean values can also be represented numerically where **True** is **1** and **False** is **0** (zero).

4 Add statements to display the results of NOT evaluations

```
print( '\nNOT Logic:' )
print( 'a =' , a , '\tnot a =' , not a )
print( 'b =' , b , '\tnot b =' , not b )
```

5 Save then run this program – to see the result of logic operations

```
Python Shell                    — □ ×
File  Edit  Shell  Debug  Options  Windows  Help
>>> ============= RESTART ============ ====
>>>
AND Logic:
a and a = True
a and b = False
b and b = False

OR Logic:
a or a = True
a or b = True
b or b = False

NOT Logic:
a = True          not a = False
b = False         not b = True
>>>|
```

Don't forget

Note that the expression **False and False** returns **False**, not **True** – perhaps demonstrating the maxim "two wrongs don't make a right".

Testing condition

Many programming languages, such as C++ or Java, have a **?:** "ternary" operator that evaluates an expression for a **True** or **False** condition then returns one of two specified values depending on the result of the evaluation. A **?:** ternary operator has this syntax:

(test-expression) ? if-true-return-this : if-false-return-this

Unlike other programming languages, Python does not have a **?:** ternary operator but has instead a "conditional expression" that works in a similar way using **if** and **else** keywords with this syntax:

if-true-return-this **if** *(test-expression)* **else** *if-false-return-this*

Although the conditional expression syntax can initially appear confusing it is well worth becoming familiar with this expression as it can execute powerful program branching with minimal code. For example, to branch when a variable is not a value of one:

if-true-do-this **if** (var != 1) **else** *if-false-do-this*

The conditional expression can be used in Python programming to assign the maximum or minimum value of two variables to a third variable. For example, to assign a minimum like this:

c = a if (a < b) else b

The expression in parentheses returns **True** when the value of variable **a** is less than that of variable **b** – so in this case the lesser value of variable **a** gets assigned to variable **c**.

Similarly, replacing the **<** less than operator in the test expression with the **>** greater than operator would assign the greater value of variable **b** to variable **c**.

Another common use of the conditional expression incorporates the **%** remainder operator in the test expression to determine if the value of a variable is an odd number or an even number:

if-true(odd)-do-this **if** (var % 2 != 0) **else** *if-false(even)-do-this*

Where the result of dividing the variable value by two does leave a remainder, the number is odd – where there is no remainder the number is even. The test expression (**var % 2 == 1**) would have the same effect but it is preferable to test for inequality – it's easier to spot when something is different than when it's identical.

44

1 Start a new program by initializing two variables with integer values for conditional evaluation
```
a = 1
b = 2
```

condition.py

2 Next, add statements to display the results of conditional evaluation – describing the first variable's value
```
print( '\nVariable a Is :' , 'One' if ( a == 1 ) else 'Not One' )
print( 'Variable a Is :' , 'Even' if ( a % 2 == 0 ) else 'Odd' )
```

3 Now, add statements to display the results of conditional evaluation – describing the second variable's value
```
print( '\nVariable b Is :' , 'One' if ( b == 1 ) else 'Not One' )
print( 'Variable b Is :' , 'Even' if ( b % 2 == 0 ) else 'Odd' )
```

4 Then, add a statement to assign the result of a conditional evaluation to a new variable
```
top = a if ( a > b ) else b
```

5 Finally, add a statement to display the assigned result – identifying the greater of the two variable values
```
print( '\nGreater Value Is:' , top )
```

6 Save then run this program – to see the result of conditional expression operations

```
                    Python Shell              –  □  ×
File  Edit  Shell  Debug  Options  Windows  Help
>>> ============= RESTART ==================
>>>

Variable a Is : One
Variable a Is : Odd

Variable b Is : Not One
Variable b Is : Even

Greater Value Is: 2
>>>|
```

Beware

You may find that some Python programmers dislike conditional expressions as they consider its syntax contradicts the principle of easy readability.

Setting order

Operator precedence determines the order in which expressions get evaluated. For example, in the expression **3 * 8 + 4** the default order of precedence determines that multiplication with the * multiply operator is completed first, so the result is 28 (24 + 4).

The table below lists Python's operator precedence in descending order – those on the top row have highest precedence; those on lower rows have successively lower precedence. The precedence of operators on the same row is chained Left-To-Right.

Don't forget

The * multiply operator is on a higher row than the + addition operator – so in the expression **3 * 8 + 4** multiplication is completed first, before the addition.

Operator:	Description:
**	Exponent
+	Positive
-	Negative
~	Bitwise NOT
*	Multiplication
/	Division
//	Floor division
%	Remainder
+	Addition
-	Subtraction
|	Bitwise OR
^	Bitwise XOR
&	Bitwise AND
>>	Bitwise right shift
<<	Bitwise left shift
>, >=, <, <=, ==, !=	Comparison
= , %= , /= , //= , -= , += , *= , **=	Assignment
is , is not	Identity
in , not in	Membership
not	Boolean NOT
and	Boolean AND
or	Boolean OR

Hot tip

Bitwise operators are used for low-level manipulation so are omitted from this book. Identity and membership operators are introduced later but are included here for completeness.

46

1. Start a new program by initializing three variables with integer values for precedence comparison
```
a = 2
b = 4
c = 8
```

order.py

2. Next, add statements to display the results of default precedence and forcing addition before multiplication
```
print( '\nDefault Order:\t', a, '*', c,'+', b, '=',  a * c + b )
print( 'Forced Order:\t', a, '* (', c,'+', b, ') =',  a * ( c + b ) )
```

3. Now, add statements to display the results of default precedence and forcing subtraction before division
```
print( '\nDefault Order:\t', c, '//', b, '-', a, '=',  c // b - a )
print( 'Forced Order:\t', c, '// (', b,'-', a, ') =', c // ( b - a ) )
```

Don't forget

The // floor division operator truncates floating point values at the decimal point – but the / division operator retains them.

4. Finally, add statements to display the results of default precedence and forcing addition before remainder operation and before exponent operation
```
print( '\nDefault Order:\t', c, '%', a, '+', b, '=',  c % a + b )
print( 'Forced Order:\t', c, '% (', a, '+', b, ') =',  c % ( a + b ) )
print( '\nDefault Order:\t', c, '**', a, '+', b, '=',  c ** a + b )
print( 'Forced Order:\t', c, '** (', a, '+', b, ') =',  c ** ( a + b ) )
```

5. Save then run this program – to see the results of default and explicit precedence

```
                          Python Shell              –  □  ×
File  Edit  Shell  Debug  Options  Windows  Help
>>> ============= RESTART =============
>>>

Default Order:       2 * 8 + 4 = 20
Forced Order:        2 * ( 8 + 4 ) = 24

Default Order:       8 // 4 – 2 = 0
Forced Order:        8 // ( 4 – 2 ) = 4

Default Order:       8 % 2 + 4 = 4
Forced Order:        8 % ( 2 + 4 ) = 2

Default Order:       8 ** 2 + 4 = 68
Forced Order:        8 ** ( 2 + 4 ) = 262144
>>>|
```

Beware

Do not rely upon default precedence – always use parentheses to clarify your expressions.

47

Summary

- Arithmetical operators can form expressions with two operands for addition **+**, subtraction -, multiplication *, division **/**, floor division **//**, remainder **%,** or exponent ******

- The **%** remainder operator is useful to determine whether a number is an odd or even value

- Floor division with the **//** operator removes any floating-point part from the result

- The assignment **=** operator can be combined with an arithmetical operator to perform an arithmetical calculation then assign its result

- The **+=** operator is useful to add a value onto an existing value stored in a variable to make a combined total value

- Comparison operators can form expressions comparing two operands for equality **==**, inequality **!=**, greater **>**, lesser **<**, greater or equal **>=**, and lesser or equal **<=** values

- Logical **and** and **or** operators form expressions evaluating two operands to return a Boolean value of **True** or **False**

- The logical **not** operator returns the inverse Boolean value of a single operand - turning **True** to **False** , and vice versa

- The not operator is useful to toggle a value between **True** and **False** on successive iterations of a loop

- A conditional **if-else** expression evaluates a given expression for a Boolean **True** or **False** value then returns one of two operands depending on its result

- Expressions containing multiple operators will execute their operations in accordance with the default precedence rules unless explicitly determined by the addition of parentheses **( )**

- Typically, addition **+** and subtraction - will be performed before multiplication * and division **/** unless explicitly specified

4 Making lists

This chapter demonstrates how to create code to store data in lists and how to retrieve data from lists.

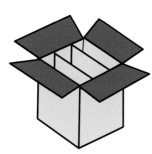

Writing lists

Some programming languages allow variables to be declared with no initial value, but in Python programming a variable must be assigned an initial value (initialized) in the statement that declares it – otherwise the interpreter will report a "not defined" error.

Multiple variables can be initialized with a common value in a single statement using a sequence of = assignments. For example, to simultaneously assign a common value to three variables:

a = b = c = 10

Alternatively, multiple variables can be initialized with differing values in a single statement using comma separators. For example, to simultaneously assign different values to three variables:

a , b , c = 1 , 2 , 3

Unlike a regular variable, which can only store a single item of data, an array variable can store multiple items of data. In Python these are known as "list" variables. The data is stored sequentially in list "elements" that are index numbered starting at zero. So the first value is stored in element zero, the second value is stored in element one, and so on. An array list is created much like any other variable but is initialized by assigning values as a comma-separated list between square brackets. For example, creating a list named "nums" like this:

nums = [0 , 1 , 2 , 3 , 4 , 5]

	[0]	[1]	[2]
[0]	1	2	3
[1]	4	5	6

A single list element can be referenced using the list name followed by square brackets containing that element's index number. This means that **nums[1]** references the second element in the example above – not the first element. As element numbering starts at zero its first element is referenced with **nums[0]**.

Lists can have more than one index – to represent multiple dimensions, rather than the single dimension of a regular list. Multi-dimensional lists of three indices and more are uncommon but two-dimensional lists are useful to store grid-based information such as X,Y coordinates.

A list of string values can even be considered to be a multi-dimensional list as each string is itself a list of characters. So each character can be referenced by its index number within its particular string.

...cont'd

1 Start a new program by initializing a list of three elements containing string values

```
quarter = [ 'January' , 'February' , 'March' ]
```

2 Next, add statements to individually display the value contained in each list element

```
print( 'First Month :' ,  quarter[0] )
print( 'Second Month :' , quarter[1] )
print( 'Third Month :' ,  quarter[2] )
```

list.py

3 Add a statement to create a multi-dimensional list of two elements, which themselves are lists that each have three elements containing integer values

```
coords = [ [ 1 , 2 , 3 ] , [ 4 , 5 , 6 ] ]
```

4 Now, add statements to display the values contained in two specific inner list elements

```
print( '\nTop Left 0,0 :' , coords[0][0] )
print( 'Bottom Right 1,2 :' , coords[1][2] )
```

String indices may also be negative numbers – to start counting from the right where -1 references the last letter.

5 Finally, add a statement to display just one character of a string value

```
print( '\nSecond Month First Letter :' , quarter[1][0] )
```

6 Save then run the program – to see the list element values get displayed

```
Python Shell                    –  □  ×
File  Edit  Shell  Debug  Options  Windows  Help
>>> ============= RESTART =============
>>>
First Month : January
Second Month : February
Third Month : March

Top Left 0,0 : 1
Bottom Right 1,2 : 6

Second Month First Letter : F
>>>
```

Loop structures, which are introduced later in this chapter, are often used to iterate through list elements.

51

Changing lists

List variables, which can contain multiple items of data, are widely used in Python programming and have various function "methods" that can be "dot-suffixed" to the list name for manipulation:

List Method:	Description:
list.append(*x*)	Adds item *x* to the end of the list
list.extend(*L*)	Adds all items in list *L* to the end of the list
list.insert(*i*,*x*)	Inserts item *x* at index position *i*
list.remove(*x*)	Removes first item *x* from the list
list.pop(*i*)	Removes item at index position *i* and returns it
list.index(*x*)	Returns the index position in the list of first item *x*
list.count(*x*)	Returns the number of times *x* appears in the list
list.sort()	Sort all list items, in place
list.reverse()	Reverse all list items, in place

Hot tip

For lists that contain both numerical and string values the **sort()** method returns the list elements sorted first numerically then alphabetically – for example as 1,2,3,A,B,C.

Python also has a useful **len(L)** function that returns the length of the list **L** as the total number of elements it contains. Like the **index()** and **count()** methods the returned value is numeric so cannot be directly concatenated to a text string for output.

String representation of numeric values can, however, be produced by Python's **str(n)** function for concatenation to other strings, which returns a string version of the numeric **n** value. Similarly, a string representation of an entire list can be returned by the **str(L)** function for concatenation to other strings. In both cases remember that the original version remains unchanged, as the returned versions are merely copies of the original version.

Hot tip

Python also has an **int(s)** function that returns a numeric version of the string **s** value.

Individual list elements can be deleted by specifying the list name and index number after the Python **del** keyword. This can remove one element at a specified *i* index position, or a "slice" of elements using slice notation *i1:i2* to specify the index number of the first and last element. In this case, *i1* is the index number of the first element to be removed and all elements up to, but not including, the element at the *i2* index number will be removed.

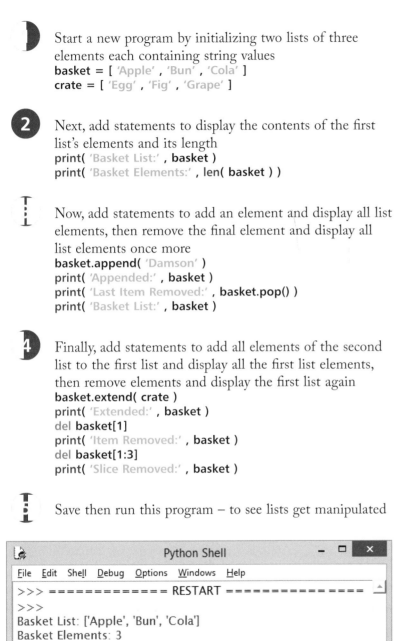

pop.py

Start a new program by initializing two lists of three elements each containing string values
```
basket = [ 'Apple' , 'Bun' , 'Cola' ]
crate = [ 'Egg' , 'Fig' , 'Grape' ]
```

2 Next, add statements to display the contents of the first list's elements and its length
```
print( 'Basket List:' , basket )
print( 'Basket Elements:' , len( basket ) )
```

Now, add statements to add an element and display all list elements, then remove the final element and display all list elements once more
```
basket.append( 'Damson' )
print( 'Appended:' , basket )
print( 'Last Item Removed:' , basket.pop() )
print( 'Basket List:' , basket )
```

4 Finally, add statements to add all elements of the second list to the first list and display all the first list elements, then remove elements and display the first list again
```
basket.extend( crate )
print( 'Extended:' , basket )
del basket[1]
print( 'Item Removed:' , basket )
del basket[1:3]
print( 'Slice Removed:' , basket )
```

Save then run this program – to see lists get manipulated

Python Shell

File Edit Shell Debug Options Windows Help
```
>>> ============== RESTART ==============
>>>
Basket List: ['Apple', 'Bun', 'Cola']
Basket Elements: 3
Appended: ['Apple', 'Bun', 'Cola', 'Damson']
Last Item Removed: Damson
Basket List: ['Apple', 'Bun', 'Cola']
Extended: ['Apple', 'Bun', 'Cola', 'Egg', 'Fig', 'Grape']
Item Removed: ['Apple', 'Cola', 'Egg', 'Fig', 'Grape']
Slice Removed: ['Apple', 'Fig', 'Grape']
>>>
```

Don't forget

The last index number in the slice denotes at what point to stop removing elements – but the element at that position does not get removed.

53

Fixing lists

The values in a regular list can be changed as the program proceeds. Each element may be assigned a replacement value using the = assignment operator to specify the list name, element index number, and the replacement value. In programming terms the values stored in a regular list are "mutable" – they can be changed. Elements can also be dynamically added to a regular list, and dynamically removed from a regular list, as the program proceeds. This means that a regular list is ideal if your program will make changes to element values.

Where a list will only contain constant values, that will never change when the program runs, a fixed list can better be created. In programming terms, the values stored in a fixed list are "immutable" – they cannot be changed. Elements cannot be dynamically added to a fixed list, or dynamically removed from a fixed list, as the program proceeds. This means that a fixed list is ideal if your program will never make changes to element values.

A restrictive immutable Python list is known as a "tuple" and is created by assigning values as a comma-separated list between parentheses in a process known as "tuple packing":

colors_tuple = ('Red' , 'Green' , 'Red' , 'Blue', 'Red')

An individual tuple element can be referenced using the tuple name followed by square brackets containing that element's index number. Usefully, all values stored inside a tuple can be assigned to individual variables in a process known as "sequence unpacking":

a , b , c , d , e = colors_tuple

Regular list methods, such as **sort()** and **reverse()**, cannot be used on tuples but the built-in Python **type()** function can be used to reveal the data class type and the built-in **len()** function can be used to return the length of the tuple.

Typically, a tuple is used to store values that are a collection of constant unchanging values such as day-of-the-week names, month-of-the-year names, or personal details of first name, last name, date-of-birth, address, phone number, etc.

Don't forget

Like index numbering, with lists the items in a tuple sequence are numbered from zero.

Beware

There must be the same number of variables as items to unpack a tuple.

54

1 Start a new program by initializing a tuple then display its class type

```
days = ( 'Mon' , 'Tue' , 'Wed' , 'Thu' , 'Fri' , 'Sat' , 'Sun' )
print( 'days:' , type( days ) )
```

tuple.py

2 Next, display the entire contents of the tuple, its length, and the value stored in its first element

```
print( 'Days of the week:' , days )
print( 'No. of days in week:' , len( days ) )
print( 'Start day of week:' , days[0] )
```

3 Now, initialize another tuple containing some personal details of a user

```
user = ( 'John' , 'Doe' , 'Paris' , '555-1234' )
```

4 Then, display the user's full name

```
print( 'Name:' , user[0] , user[1] )
```

5 Finally, display the user's phone number

```
print( 'Phone:' , user[3] )
```

6 Save then run this program – to see the tuple values

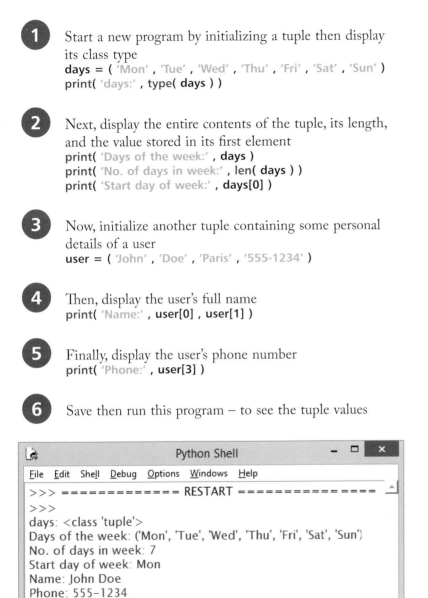

Hot tip

A tuple may contain items that are not unique to its other elements.

Setting lists

The values in a regular list or a fixed list tuple can be repeated in its elements, but a list of unique values can be created where duplication is not allowed. A restrictive Python list of unique values is known as a "set" and is created by assigning values as a comma-separated list between curly brackets (braces) like this:

phonetic_set = { 'Alpha' , 'Bravo' , 'Charlie' }

Unlike regular lists or tuples, individual elements in a set cannot be referenced using the set name followed by square brackets containing an index number. Instead, sets have powerful methods that can be dot-suffixed to the set name for manipulation and comparison of values:

Hot tip

A set may not contain items that are not unique to its other elements.

Set Method:	Description:
set.add(*x*)	Adds item *x* to the set
set.update(*x,y,z*)	Adds multiple items to the set
set.copy()	Returns a copy of the set
set.pop()	Removes one random item from the set
set.discard(*i*)	Removes item at position *i* from the set
set1.intersection(*set2*)	Returns items that appear in both sets
set1.difference(*set2*)	Returns items in *set1* but not in *set2*

Don't forget

More set methods can be found in the Python documentation online at **docs.python.org**

The built-in Python **type()** function can be used to reveal the data class type and the built-in **len()** function can be used to return the length of the set. Additionally, the Python built-in membership operator **in** can be used to find values in a set.

Typically, a set is used to store unique values that are a collection of changeable values, which can easily be searched and compared using the powerful set methods. Although you cannot access set element values by index, a set can be converted to a regular list using the Python built-in **list()** function to allow element access.

set.py

Start a new program by initializing a set with unique name values then display its class type
```python
party_goers = { 'Andrew' , 'Barbara' , 'Carole' , 'David' }
print( 'party_goers:' , type( party_goers ) )
```

Next, add statements to search the set elements for two specified values
```python
print( 'Did David go to the party?' , 'David' in party_goers )
print( 'Did Kelly go to the party?' , 'Kelly' in party_goers )
```

Now, initialize another set with unique name values
```python
students = { 'Andrew' , 'Kelly' , 'Lynn' , 'David' }
```

Then, create a further set containing only common values that appear in both previous sets
```python
commons = party_goers.intersection( students )
```

Initialize a regular list of the common values – so the elements values can be individually accessed
```python
party_students = list( commons )
```

Finally, display all common values and the value stored in the first regular list element
```python
print( 'Students at the party:' , party_students )
print( 'First student at the party:' , party_students[0] )
```

Save then run this program – to see the set values

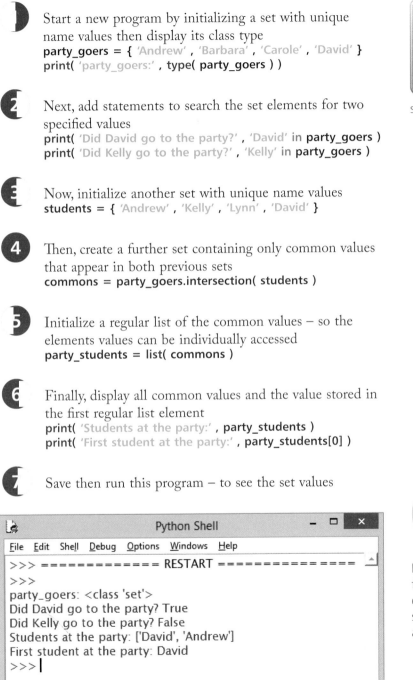

```
Python Shell                                    _  □  ×
File  Edit  Shell  Debug  Options  Windows  Help
>>> ============= RESTART ============ ====
>>>
party_goers: <class 'set'>
Did David go to the party? True
Did Kelly go to the party? False
Students at the party: ['David', 'Andrew']
First student at the party: David
>>> |
```

Beware

Notice that the **list()** function may not place element values in the same order as they appear in the set.

Naming elements

In Python programming a "dictionary" is a data container that can store multiple items of data as a list of key:value pairs. Unlike regular list container values, which are referenced by their index number, values stored in dictionaries are referenced by their associated key. The key must be unique within that dictionary and is typically a string name, although numbers may be used.

Creating a dictionary is simply a matter of assigning the key:value pairs as a comma-separated list between curly brackets (braces) to a name of your choice. Strings must be enclosed within quotes, as usual, and a : colon character must come between the key and its associated value.

A key:value pair can be deleted from a dictionary by specifying the dictionary name and the pair's key to the **del** keyword. Conversely, a key:value pair can be added to a dictionary by assigning a value to the dictionary's name and a new key.

Python dictionaries have a **keys()** method that can be dot-suffixed to the dictionary name to return a list, in random order, of all the keys in that dictionary. If you prefer the keys to be sorted into alphanumeric order, simply enclose the statement within the parentheses of the Python **sorted()** function.

A dictionary can be searched to see if it contains a particular key with the Python **in** operator, using the syntax *key* **in** *dictionary*. The search will return a Boolean **True** value when the key is found in the specified dictionary, otherwise it will return **False**.

Dictionaries are the final type of data container available in Python programming. In summary, the various types are:

- **Variable** – stores a single value
- **List** – stores multiple values in an ordered index array
- **Tuple** – stores multiple fixed values in a sequence
- **Set** – stores multiple unique values in an unordered collection
- **Dictionary** – stores multiple unordered key:value pairs

Hot tip

In other programming languages a list is often called an "array" and a dictionary is often called an "associative array".

Hot tip

Data is frequently associated as key:value pairs – for example, when you submit a web form a text value typed into an input field is typically associated with that text field's name as its key.

1 Start a new program by initializing a dictionary then display its data class type and its key:value contents
```
info = { 'name' : 'Bob' , 'ref' : 'Python' , 'sys' : 'Win' }
print( 'info:' , type( info ) )
print( 'Dictionary:' , info )
```

dict.py

2 Next, display a single value referenced by its key
```
print( '\nReference:' , info[ 'ref' ] )
```

3 Now, display all keys within the dictionary
```
print( '\nKeys:' , info.keys() )
```

4 Delete one pair from the dictionary and add a replacement pair then display the new key:value contents
```
del info[ 'name' ]
info[ 'user' ] = 'Tom'
print( '\nDictionary:' , info )
```

5 Finally, search the dictionary for a specific key and display the result of the search
```
print( '\nIs There A name Key?:' ,'name' in info )
```

6 Save the file then run this program – to see the dictionary keys and values

```
Python Shell
File  Edit  Shell  Debug  Options  Windows  Help
>>> ============= RESTART ===============
>>>
info: <class 'dict'>
Dictionary: {'ref': 'Python', 'sys': 'Win', 'name': 'Bob'}

Reference: Python

Keys: dict_keys(['ref', 'sys', 'name'])

Dictionary: {'ref': 'Python', 'sys': 'Win', 'user': 'Tom'}

Is There A name Key?: False
>>>
```

Beware

Notice that quotes within a string must be preceded by a backslash escape character – to prevent the string being prematurely terminated.

Summary

- Multiple variables can be initialized in a single statement using a sequence of = assignments
- A Python list is an array variable that can store multiple items of data in sequentially numbered elements that start at zero
- Data stored in a list element can be referenced using the list name followed by an index number in **[ ]** square brackets
- A list element can have more than one index to represent multiple dimensions, such as X and Y coordinates
- List variables have a number of methods that can be dot-suffixed to the list name for manipulation
- The **len()** function returns the length of a specified list
- An individual list element can be deleted by specifying the list name and element index number to the Python **del** keyword
- A Python tuple is an immutable list whose values can be assigned to individual variables by "sequence unpacking"
- Data stored in a tuple element can be referenced using the tuple name followed by an index number in **[ ]** square brackets
- A Python set is an ordered collection of unique elements whose values can be compared and manipulated by its methods
- Data stored in a set cannot be referenced by its index number
- Set variables have methods that can be dot-suffixed to the list name for manipulation and comparison
- The Python built-in membership **in** operator can be used to seek a value within a set
- A set can be converted to a regular list using the **list()** function to allow reference of element data by index number
- A Python dictionary is a list of key:value pairs of data in which each key must be unique
- Data stored in a dictionary element can be referenced using the dictionary name followed by its key in **[ ]** square brackets

5 Controlling blocks

This chapter demonstrates

how to create code to control

the flow of your programs.

Branching choices

As in many programming languages the Python **if** keyword performs a basic conditional test that evaluates a given expression for a Boolean value of **True** or **False**. This allows a program to proceed in different directions according to the result of the test and is known as "conditional branching".

In Python, the tested expression must be followed by a : colon, then statements to execute when the test succeeds should follow below on separate lines and each line must be indented from the **if** test line. The size of the indentation is not important but it must be the same for each line. So the syntax looks like this:

if *test-expression* :
      statements-to-execute-when-test-expression-is-True
      statements-to-execute-when-test-expression-is-True

The **if: elif: else:** sequence is the Python equivalent of the **switch** or **case** statements found in other languages.

Optionally, an **if** test can offer alternative statements to execute when the test fails by appending an **else** keyword after the statements to be executed when the test succeeds. The **else** keyword must be followed by a : colon and aligned with the **if** keyword but its statements must be indented in a likewise manner, so its syntax looks like this:

if *test-expression* :
      statements-to-execute-when-test-expression-is-True
      statements-to-execute-when-test-expression-is-True
else :
      statements-to-execute-when-test-expression-is-False
      statements-to-execute-when-test-expression-is-False

An **if** test block can be followed by an alternative test using the **elif** keyword ("else if") that offers statements to be executed when the alternative test succeeds. This, too, must be aligned with the **if** keyword, followed by a : colon, and its statements indented. A final **else** keyword can then be added to offer alternative statements to execute when the test fails. The syntax for the complete **if-elif-else** structure looks like this:

if *test-expression-1* :
      statements-to-execute-when-test-expression-1-is-True
      statements-to-execute-when-test-expression-1-is-True
elif *test-expression-2* :
      statements-to-execute-when-test-expression-2-is-True
      statements-to-execute-when-test-expression-2-is-True
else :
      statements-to-execute-when-test-expressions-are-False
      statements-to-execute-when-test-expressions-are-False

Beware

Indentation of code is very important in Python as it identifies code blocks to the interpreter – other programming languages use bracketing such as { } braces.

1 Start a new program by initializing a variable with user input of an integer value
```
num = int( input( 'Please Enter A Number: ' ) )
```

if.py

2 Next, test the variable and display an appropriate response
```
if num > 5 :
        print( 'Number Exceeds 5' )
elif num < 5 :
        print( 'Number is Less Than 5' )
else :
        print( 'Number Is 5' )
```

3 Now, test the variable again using two expressions and display a response only upon success
```
if num > 7 and num < 9 :
        print( 'Number is 8' )
if num == 1 or num == 3 :
        print( 'Number Is 1 or 3' )
```

The user input is read as a string value by default so must be cast as an **int** data type with **int()** for arithmetical comparison.

4 Save then run the program – to see conditional branching in action

```
┌─────────────────────────────────────────┐
│  ⏻            Python Shell       ─  □  ✕  │
├─────────────────────────────────────────┤
│ File  Edit  Shell  Debug  Options  Windows  Help │
├─────────────────────────────────────────┤
│ >>> ============= RESTART =============  │
│ >>>                                      │
│ Please Enter A Number: 4                 │
│ Number is Less Than 5                    │
│ >>> ============= RESTART =============  │
│ >>>                                      │
│ Please Enter A Number: 6                 │
│ Number Exceeds 5                         │
│ >>> ============= RESTART =============  │
│ >>>                                      │
│ Please Enter A Number: 5                 │
│ Number Is 5                              │
│ >>> ============= RESTART =============  │
│ >>>                                      │
│ Please Enter A Number: 3                 │
│ Number is Less Than 5                    │
│ Number Is 1 or 3                         │
│ >>>                                      │
└─────────────────────────────────────────┘
```

The **and** keyword ensures the evaluation is **True** only when both tests succeed, whereas the **or** keyword ensures the evaluation is **True** when either test succeeds.

Counting loops

As in other programming languages, the Python **for** keyword loops over all items in any list specified to the **in** keyword. In Python, this statement must end with a : colon character and statements to be executed on each iteration of the loop must be indented:

for *each-item* **in** *list-name* :
      statements-to-execute-on-each-iteration
      statements-to-execute-on-each-iteration

Because a string is simply a list of characters, the **for in** statement can loop over each character. Similarly, a **for in** statement can loop over each element in a list, each item in a tuple, each member of a set, or each key in a dictionary.

The **for** loop in Python is unlike that in other languages, such as C as it does not allow step size and end to be specified.

A **for in** loop iterates over the items of any list or string in the order that they appear in the sequence but you cannot directly specify the number of iterations to make, a halting condition, or the size of iteration step. You can, however, use the Python **range()** function to iterate over a sequence of numbers by specifying a numeric end value within its parentheses. This will generate a sequence that starts at zero and continues up to, but not including, the specified end value. For example, **range(5)** generates 0,1,2,3,4.

Optionally, you can specify both a start and end value within the parentheses of the **range()** function, separated by a comma. For example, **range(1,5)** generates 1,2,3,4. Also, you can specify a start value, end value, and a step value to the **range()** function as a comma-separated list within its parentheses. For example, **range(1,14,4)** generates 1,5,9,13.

You can specify the list's name within the parentheses of Python's **enumerate()** function to display each element's index number and its associated value.

The **range()** function can generate a sequence that decreases, counting down, as well as those that count upward.

When looping through multiple lists simultaneously, the element values of the same index number in each list can be displayed together by specifying the list names as a comma-separated list within the parentheses of Python's **zip()** function.

When looping through a dictionary, you can display each key and its associated value using the dictionary **items()** method and specifying two comma-separated variable names to the **for** keyword – one for the key name and the other for its value.

1 Start a new program by initializing a regular list, a fixed
tuple list, and an associative dictionary list

```
chars = [ 'A' , 'B', 'C' ]
fruit = ( 'Apple' , 'Banana' , 'Cherry' )
info = { 'name' : 'Mike' , 'ref' : 'Python' , 'sys' : 'Win' }
```

for.py

2 Next, add statements to display all list element values

```
print( 'Elements: \t' , end = ' ' )
for item in chars :
        print( item , end = ' ' )
```

3 Now, add statements to display all list element values and
their relative index number

```
print( '\nEnumerated:\t' , end = ' ' )
for item in enumerate( chars ) :
        print( item , end = ' ' )
```

4 Then, add statements to display all list and tuple elements

```
print( '\nZipped:   \t' , end = ' ' )
for item in zip( chars , fruit ) :
        print( item , end = ' ' )
```

5 Finally, add statements to display all dictionary key names
and associated element values

```
print( '\nPaired:' )
for key , value in info.items() :
        print( key , '=' , value )
```

6 Save then run the program – to see the items displayed by
the loop iterations

```
Python Shell                    – □ ×
File  Edit  Shell  Debug  Options  Windows  Help
>>> ============= RESTART =============
>>>
Elements:          A B C
Enumerated:        (0, 'A') (1, 'B') (2, 'C')
Zipped:            ('A', 'Apple') ('B', 'Banana') ('C', 'Cherry')
Paired:
name = Mike
ref = Python
sys = Win
>>>
```

Hot tip

In programming terms,
anything that contains
multiple items that
can be looped over is
described as "iterable".

Looping conditions

A loop is a piece of code in a program that automatically repeats. One complete execution of all statements within a loop is called an "iteration" or a "pass". The length of the loop is controlled by a conditional test made within the loop. While the tested expression is found to be **True**, the loop will continue – until the tested expression is found to be **False**, at which point the loop ends.

In Python programming, the **while** keyword creates a loop. It is followed by the test expression then a : colon character. Statements to execute when the test succeeds follow below on separate lines, each line indented from the **while** test line. Importantly, the loop statement block must include a statement that will change the result of the test expression evaluation – otherwise an infinite loop is created.

Indentation of code blocks must also be observed in Python's interactive mode – like this example that produces a Fibonacci sequence of numbers from a **while** loop:

Don't forget

Unlike other Python keywords, the keywords **True** and **False** begin with uppercase letters.

```
Python Shell
File  Edit  Shell  Debug  Options  Windows  Help
>>> a = b = 1
>>> while b < 100 :
        print( b )
        a , b = b , a + b
1
2
3
5
8
13
21
34
55
89
>>>
```

Hot tip

The interactive Python interpreter automatically indents and waits when it expects further code statements from you.

Loops can be nested, one within another, to allow complete execution of all iterations of an inner nested loop on each iteration of the outer loop. A "counter" variable can be initialized with a starting value immediately before each loop definition, included in the test expression, and incremented on each iteration until the test fails – at which point the loop ends.

1 Start a new program by initializing a "counter" variable and define an outer loop using the counter variable in its test expression

```
i = 1
while i < 4 :
```

while.py

2 Next, add <u>indented</u> statements to display the counter's value and increment its value on each iteration of the loop

```
        print( 'Outer Loop Iteration:' , i )
        i += 1
```

3 Now, (still indented) initialize a second "counter" variable and define an inner loop using this variable in its test expression

```
        j = 1
        while j < 4 :
```

Hot tip

The output printed from the inner loop is indented from that of the outer loop by the **\t** tab character.

4 Finally, add <u>further-indented</u> statements to display this counter's value and increment its value on each iteration

```
                print( '\tInner Loop Iteration:' , j )
                j += 1
```

5 Save then run this program – to see the output displayed on each loop iteration

```
>>> ============== RESTART ===============
>>>
Outer Loop Iteration: 1
        Inner Loop Iteration: 1
        Inner Loop Iteration: 2
        Inner Loop Iteration: 3
Outer Loop Iteration: 2
        Inner Loop Iteration: 1
        Inner Loop Iteration: 2
        Inner Loop Iteration: 3
Outer Loop Iteration: 3
        Inner Loop Iteration: 1
        Inner Loop Iteration: 2
        Inner Loop Iteration: 3
>>>
```

Hot tip

The += assignment statement **i += 1** is simply a shorthand way to say **i = i+1** – you can also use ***= /= -=** shorthand to assign values to variables.

Skipping loops

The Python **break** keyword can be used to prematurely terminate a loop when a specified condition is met. The **break** statement is situated inside the loop statement block and is preceded by a test expression. When the test returns **True**, the loop ends immediately and the program proceeds on to the next task. For example, in a nested inner loop it proceeds to the next iteration of the outer loop.

nest.py

 Start a new program with a statement creating a loop that iterates three times
for i in range(1, 4) :

 Next, add an indented statement creating a "nested" inner loop that also iterates three times
for j in range(1, 4) :

3 Now, add a further-indented statement in the inner loop to display the counter numbers (of both the outer loop and the inner loop) on each iteration of the inner loop
print('Running i=' **, i ,** ' j=' **, j)**

4 Save then run this program – to see the counter values on each loop iteration

```
                                                       _  □  ×
                         Python Shell
File  Edit  Shell  Debug  Options  Windows  Help
>>> ============= RESTART ==============
>>>
Running i = 1  j = 1
Running i = 1  j = 2
Running i = 1  j = 3
Running i = 2  j = 1
Running i = 2  j = 2
Running i = 2  j = 3
Running i = 3  j = 1
Running i = 3  j = 2
Running i = 3  j = 3
>>> |
```

Hot tip

Compare these nested **for** loops with the nested **while** loops example on page 67.

5 Insert a **break** statement at the start of the inner loop to break from that loop – then run the program again

```
if i == 2 and j == 1 :
    print( 'Breaks inner loop at i=2 j=1' )
    break
```

```
Python Shell                               – □ ×
File  Edit  Shell  Debug  Options  Windows  Help
>>> ============== RESTART =============== ▲
>>>
Running i = 1  j = 1
Running i = 1  j = 2
Running i = 1  j = 3
Breaks inner loop at i=2 j=1
Running i = 3  j = 1
Running i = 3  j = 2
Running i = 3  j = 3
>>> |
```

break.py

The **break** statement halts all three iterations of the inner loop when the outer loop runs it for the second time.

69

The Python **continue** keyword can be used to skip a single iteration of a loop when a specified condition is met. The **continue** statement is situated inside the loop statement block and is preceded by a test expression. When the test returns **True**, that one iteration ends and the program proceeds to the next iteration.

6 Now, insert a **continue** statement at the start of the inner loop block to skip the first iteration of that loop – then run the program once more

```
if i == 1 and j == 1 :
    print( 'Continues inner loop at i=1 j=1' )
    continue
```

```
Python Shell                               – □ ×
File  Edit  Shell  Debug  Options  Windows  Help
>>> ============== RESTART =============== ▲
>>>
Continues inner loop at i=1 j=1
Running i = 1  j = 2
Running i = 1  j = 3
Breaks inner loop at i=2 j=1
Running i = 3  j = 1
Running i = 3  j = 2
Running i = 3  j = 3
>>> |
```

continue.py

The **continue** statement skips the first iteration of the inner loop when the outer loop first runs it.

Catching errors

Sections of a program in which it is possible to anticipate errors, such as those handling user input, can typically be enclosed in a **try except** block to handle "exception errors". The statements to be executed are grouped in a **try** : block and exceptions are passed to the ensuing **except** : block for handling. Optionally, this may be followed by a **finally** : block containing statements to be executed after exceptions have been handled.

Python recognizes many built-in exceptions such as the **NameError** which occurs when a variable name is not found, the **IndexError** which occurs when trying to address a non-existent list index, and the **ValueError** which occurs when a built-in operation or function receives an inappropriate value.

Each exception returns a descriptive message that can usefully be assigned to a variable with the **as** keyword. This can then be used to display the nature of the exception when it occurs.

try.py

 Start a new program by initializing a variable with a string value
title = 'Coding for Beginners In Easy Steps'

 Next, add a **try** statement block that attempts to display the variable value – but specifies the name incorrectly
try :
       print(titel)

3 Now, add an **except** statement block to display an error message when a **NameError** occurs
except NameError as msg :
       print(msg)

4 Save then run the program – to see how the error gets handled

Hot tip

In some programming languages this structure is known as try-catch exception handling.

```
                    Python Shell              _ □ ✕
File  Edit  Shell  Debug  Options  Windows  Help
>>> ============= RESTART =============
>>>
name 'titel' is not defined
>>>|
```

...cont'd

Multiple exceptions can be handled by specifying their type as a comma-separated list in parentheses within the except block:

```
except ( NameError , IndexError ) as msg :
        print( msg )
```

You can also compel the interpreter to report an exception by using the **raise** keyword to specify the type of exception to be recognized and a custom descriptive message in parentheses.

1 Start a new Python script by initializing a variable with an integer value
```
day = 32
```

raise.py

2 Next, add a **try** statement block that tests the variable value then specifies an exception and custom message
```
try :
        if day > 31 :
                raise ValueError( 'Invalid Day Number' )
        # More statements to execute get added here.
```

3 Now, add an **except** statement block to display an error message when a **ValueError** occurs
```
except ValueError as msg :
        print( 'The Program found An' , msg )
```

4 Then, add a **finally** statement block to display a message after the exception has been handled successfully
```
finally :
        print( 'But Today Is Beautiful Anyway.' )
```

5 Save then run the program – to see the raised error get handled

Statements in the **try** block are all executed unless or until an exception occurs.

```
Python Shell                    _ □ ✕
File  Edit  Shell  Debug  Options  Windows  Help
>>> ============ RESTART ============
>>>
The Program Found An Invalid Day Number
But Today Is Beautiful Anyway.
>>>
```

Summary

- The **if** keyword performs a conditional test on an expression for a Boolean value of **True** or **False**

- Conditional branching provides alternatives to an **if** test with the **else** and **elif** keywords

- Python tested expressions must be followed by a : colon character and statement blocks be indented from the test line

- A **for in** loop iterates over each item in a specified list or string

- Python **for in** loop statements must be followed by a : colon character and statement blocks be indented from the statement

- The **range()** function generates a numerical sequence that can be used to specify the length of a **for in** loop

- The **enumerate()** function can specify the name of a list to display each element index number and its stored value

- The **zip()** function can display the stored values of the same index number in multiple lists

- A **while** loop repeats while an initial test expression remains **True** and ends when that test expression becomes **False**

- Python **while** loop statements must be followed by a : colon character and statement blocks be indented from the statement

- The value of a counter variable can be tested in a test expression to control the number of loop iterations

- The **break** keyword can be used to test an expression for a **True** value and immediately exit a loop when the test returns **False**

- The **continue** keyword can be used to test an expression for a **True** value and exit a single iteration when the test returns **False**

- Anticipated runtime exception errors can be handled by enclosing statements in a **try except** block

- Optionally, a **finally** statement can be used to specify statements to be executed after exceptions have been handled

- Python **try, except,** and **finally** statements must be followed by a : colon and statement blocks be indented from the statement

6 Creating functions

This chapter demonstrates how to code re-usable blocks of code in your programs.

Defining blocks

Previous examples in this book have used built-in functions of the Python programming language, such as the **print()** function. However, most programs have a number of coder-defined custom functions that can be called as required when the program runs.

A custom Python function is created using the **def** (definition) keyword followed by a name of your choice and **( )** parentheses. The coder can choose any name for a function except the keywords of the programming language and the name of an existing built-in function. This line must end with a : colon character, then the statements to be executed whenever the function gets called must appear on lines below and indented. Syntax of a function definition, therefore, looks like this:

def *function-name* **( ) :**
    statements-to-be-executed
    statements-to-be-executed

Function statements must be indented from the definition line by the same amount so the Python interpreter can recognize the block.

Once the function statements have been executed, program flow resumes at the point directly following the function call. This modularity is very useful in programming to isolate set routines so they can be called upon repeatedly.

To create custom functions it is necessary to understand the accessibility ("scope") of variables in a program:

- Variables created outside functions can be referenced by statements inside functions – they have "global" scope
- Variables created inside functions cannot be referenced from outside the function in which they have been created – these have "local" scope

The limited accessibility of local variables means that variables of the same name can appear in different functions without conflict.

Avoid using global variables in order to prevent accidental conflict – use only local variables where possible.

If you want to coerce a local variable to make it accessible elsewhere it must first be declared with the Python **global** keyword followed by its name only. It may subsequently be assigned a value that can be referenced from anywhere in the program. Where a global variable and a local variable have the same name, the function will use the local version.

Start a new program by initializing a global variable
global_var = 1

Next, create a function named "my_vars" to display the value contained within the global variable
def my_vars() :
    print('Global variable:' , global_var)

def.py

Now, add indented statements to the function block to initialize a local variable and display the value it contains
    local_var = 2
    print('Local variable:' , local_var)

Then, add indented statements to the function block to create a coerced global variable and assign an initial value
    global inner_var
    inner_var = 3

Add a statement after the function to call upon that function to execute the statements it contains
my_vars()

Finally, add a statement to display the value contained in the coerced global variable
print('Coerced Global:' , inner_var)

Save then run the program – to see the custom function display the variable values

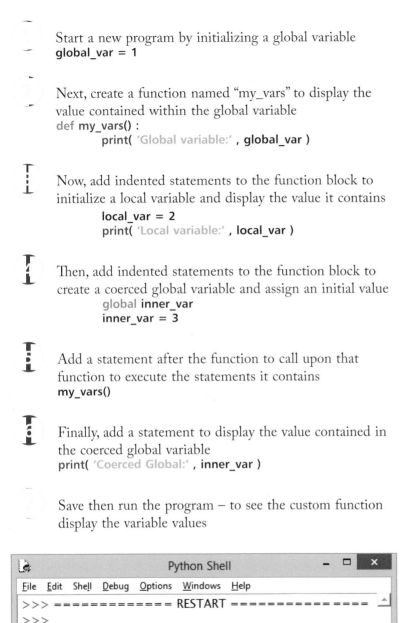

```
Python Shell                          –  □  ×
File  Edit  Shell  Debug  Options  Windows  Help
>>> ============= RESTART =============
>>>
Global variable: 1
Local variable: 2
Co-erced Global variable: 3
>>> |
```

75

Hot tip

Variables that are not global but appear in some outer scope can be addressed using the **nonlocal** keyword.

Adding parameters

When defining a custom function in a program you may optionally specify a "parameter" name between the function's parentheses. An "argument" value can then be passed to that parameter by specifying the value in the parentheses of the call to the function. The function can now use that passed in value during its execution by referencing it via the parameter name. For example, defining a function to accept a parameter to print out:

def echo(user) :
      print('User:' , user)

A call to this function must specify an argument value to be passed to the parameter in its parentheses so it can be printed out:

echo('Mike')

Multiple parameters can be specified in the function definition by including a comma-separated list of parameter names within the function parentheses:

def echo(user , lang , sys) :
      print(User:' , user , 'Language:' , lang , 'Platform:' , sys)

When calling a function whose definition specifies parameters, the call must include the same number of arguments as parameters. For example, to call this example with multiple parameters:

echo('Mike' , 'Python' , 'Windows')

The passed values must appear in the same order as the parameter list unless the caller also specifies the parameter names like this:

echo(lang = 'Python' , user = 'Mike' , sys = 'Windows')

Optionally, a default value may be specified in the parameter list when defining a function. This will be overridden when the caller specifies a value for that parameter but will be used by the function when no argument value gets passed by the caller:

def echo(user , lang , sys = 'Linux') :
      print(User:' , user , 'Language:' , lang , 'Platform:' , sys)

This means you may call the function passing fewer values than the number of parameters specified in the function definition, to use the default parameter value, or pass the same number of values as specified parameters to override the default value.

Parameters are special variables for internal use only within a function – they must adhere to the same naming rules as regular variables.

Name parameters the same as variables passed to them to make the data movement obvious.

1 Start a new program by defining a function with three parameters that will print out passed-in argument values
```python
def echo( user , lang , sys ) :
        print( 'User:', user, 'Language:', lang, 'Platform:', sys )
```

param.py

2 Next, call the function passing string argument values to the function parameters in the order they appear
```python
echo( 'Mike' , 'Python' , 'Windows' )
```

3 Now, call the function passing string arguments to the function parameters by specifying the parameter names
```python
echo( lang = 'Python' , sys = 'Mac OS' , user = 'Anne' )
```

4 Then, define another function with two parameters having default values that will print out parameter values
```python
def mirror( user = 'Carole' , lang = 'Python' ) :
        print( '\nUser:' , user , 'Language:' , lang )
```

5 Finally, add statements to call the second function both using and overriding default values
```python
mirror()
mirror( lang = 'Java' )
mirror( user = 'Tony' )
mirror( 'Susan' , 'C++' )
```

6 Save then run the program – to see the function display the argument values or default parameter values

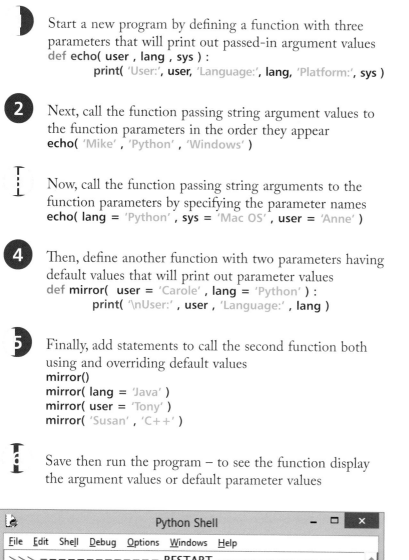

```
Python Shell                          _  □  ✕
File  Edit  Shell  Debug  Options  Windows  Help
>>> ============= RESTART ================
>>>
User: Mike Language: Python Platform: Windows
User: Anne Language: Python Platform: Mac OS

User: Carole Language: Python

User: Carole Language: Java

User: Tony Language: Python

User: Susan Language: C++
>>>
```

Hot tip

Arguments are the actual data values passed to function parameters by the function call.

Returning results

Like Python's built-in **str()** function, which returns a string representation of the value specified as its argument by the caller, your custom functions can also return a value to their caller by using the **return** keyword to specify a value to be returned. For example, to return to the caller the total of adding two specified parameter values like this:

```
def sum( a , b ) :
        return a + b
```

The returned result may be assigned to a variable by the caller for subsequent use by the program like this:

```
total = sum( 8 , 4 )
print( 'Eight Plus Four Is:' , total )
```

Or the returned result may be used directly "in-line" like this:

```
print( 'Eight Plus Four Is:' , sum( 8 , 4 ) )
```

Typically, a **return** statement will appear at the very end of a function block to return the final result of executing all statements contained in that function.

A **return** statement may, however, appear earlier in the function block to halt execution of all subsequent statements in that block. This immediately resumes execution of the program at the caller. Optionally, the **return** statement may specify a value to be returned to the caller or the value may be omitted. Where no value is specified, a default value of **None** is assumed. Typically, this is used to halt execution of the function statements after a conditional test is found to be **False**. For example, where a passed argument value is below a specified number:

```
def sum( a , b ) :
        if a < 5 :
                return
        return a + b
```

In this case, the function will return the default value **None** when the first passed argument value is below five and the final statement will not be executed.

Where the function is to perform arithmetic, user input can be validated for integer values with the built-in **isdigit()** function.

Don't forget

You can specify a default value for a parameter in the function definition.

...cont'd

Start a new program by initializing a variable with user
input of an integer value for manipulation

```
num = input( 'Enter An Integer:' )
```

return.py

Next, add a function definition that accepts a single
argument value to be passed from the caller

```
def square( num ) :
```

Now, insert into the function block an indented statement
to validate the passed argument value as an integer or halt
further execution of the function's statements

```
if not num.isdigit() :
    return 'Invalid Entry'
```

Then, add indented statements to cast the passed
argument value as an **int** data type then return the sum of
squaring that value to the caller

```
num = int( num )
return num * num
```

Finally, add a statement to output a string and the
returned value from the function call

```
print( num , 'Squared Is:' , square( num ) )
```

Save then run the program – to see the function display
the returned values

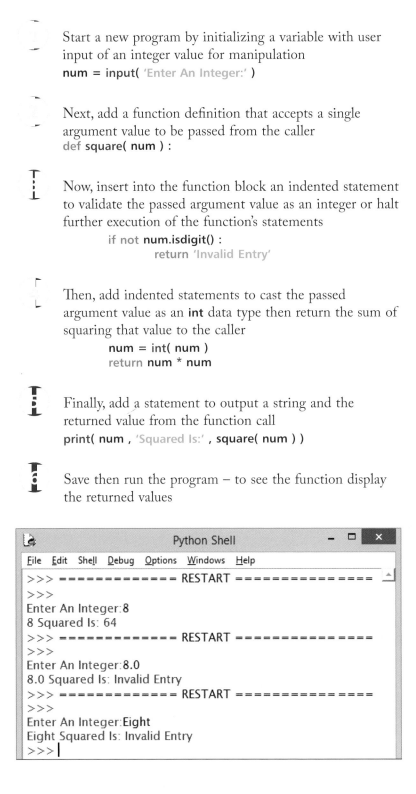

```
┌─────────────────────────────────────────────────┐
│ 🖳                  Python Shell      –  □   ✕    │
├─────────────────────────────────────────────────┤
│ File  Edit  Shell  Debug  Options  Windows  Help │
│ >>> ============= RESTART ============ ===       │
│ >>>                                              │
│ Enter An Integer:8                               │
│ 8 Squared Is: 64                                 │
│ >>> ============= RESTART ============ ====      │
│ >>>                                              │
│ Enter An Integer:8.0                             │
│ 8.0 Squared Is: Invalid Entry                    │
│ >>> ============= RESTART ============ ====      │
│ >>>                                              │
│ Enter An Integer:Eight                           │
│ Eight Squared Is: Invalid Entry                  │
│ >>>                                              │
└─────────────────────────────────────────────────┘
```

Beware

Remember that user
input is read as a **str**
data type – so must be
cast into an **int** or **float**
data type for arithmetic.

Storing functions

Function definitions can usefully be stored in one or more separate files for easier maintenance and to allow them to be used in several programs without copying the definitions into each one. Each Python file storing function definitions is called a "module" and the module name is the file name without the ".py" extension.

Functions stored in the module are made available to a program using the Python **import** keyword followed by the module name. Although not essential, it is customary to put any **import** statements at the beginning of the program.

Imported functions can be called using their name dot suffixed after the module name. For example, a "steps" function from an imported module named "ineasy" can be called with **ineasy.steps()**.

Where functions stored in a module include parameters, it is often useful to assign a default value to the parameter in the definition. This makes the function more versatile as it becomes optional for the call to specify a parameter value.

 Start a new module by defining a function that supplies a default string value to its parameter for display
```
def purr( pet = 'A Cat' ) :
        print( pet , 'Says MEOW!' )
```

 Next, add two more function definitions that also supply default string values to their parameters for display
```
def lick( pet = 'A Cat' ) :
        print( pet , 'Drinks Milk' )

def nap( pet = 'A Cat' ) :
        print( pet , 'Sleeps By The Fire' )
```

cat.py

 Now, save the file as "cat.py" so the module is named "cat"

4 Start a new program with a statement to make the "cat" module functions available
```
import cat
```

5 Next, call each function without supplying an argument
```
cat.purr()
cat.lick()
cat.nap()
```

kitty.py

Now, call each function again and pass an argument to each then save the file
cat.purr('Kitty' **)**
cat.lick('Kitty' **)**
cat.nap('Kitty' **)**

 Start another program by making the "cat" module functions available once more
import cat

tiger.py

8 Then request the user enters a name to overwrite the default parameter value
pet = input('Enter A Pet Name: ' **)**

 Finally, call each function passing the user-defined value as the argument
cat.purr(pet)
cat.lick(pet)
cat.nap(pet)

10 Save then run these programs – to see output from the imported module in each program

```
Python Shell                          –  □  ×
File  Edit  Shell  Debug  Options  Windows  Help
>>> ============= RESTART ============ ====
>>>
A Cat Says MEOW!
A Cat Drinks Milk
A Cat Sleeps By The Fire
Kitty Says MEOW!
Kitty Drinks Milk
Kitty Sleeps By The Fire
>>> ============= RESTART ============ ====
>>>
Enter A Pet Name: Tiger
Tiger Says MEOW!
Tiger Drinks Milk
Tiger Sleeps By The Fire
>>> |
```

You can create an alias when importing a module using **import as** keywords. For example, **import cat as tom** allows you to use **tom** as the function prefix in calls.

Importing functions

Internally, each Python module and program has its own "symbol table" which is used by all functions defined in that context only. This avoids possible conflicts with functions of the same name in another module if both modules were imported into one program.

When you import a module with an **import** statement, that module's symbol table does not get added to the program's symbol table – only the module's name gets added. That is why you need to call the module's functions using their module name prefix. Importing a "steps" function from a module named "ineasy" and another "steps" function from a module named "dance" means they can be called without conflict as **ineasy.steps()** and **dance.steps()**.

Generally, it is preferable to avoid conflicts by importing the module name and calling its functions with the module name prefix, but you can import individual function names instead with a **from import** statement. The module name is specified after the **from** keyword, and functions to import are specified as a comma-separated list after the **import** keyword. Alternatively, the * wildcard character can be specified after **import** to import all function names into the program's own symbol table. This means the functions can be called without a module name prefix.

Don't forget

Where you import individual function names, the module name does not get imported – so it cannot be used as a prefix.

dog.py

pooch.py

1 Start a new module by defining a function that supplies a default string value to its parameter
```
def bark( pet = 'A Dog' ) :
        print( pet , 'Says WOOF!' )
```

2 Next, add two more function definitions that also supply default string values to their parameters
```
def lick( pet = 'A Dog' ) :
        print( pet , 'Drinks water' )

def nap( pet = 'A Dog' ) :
        print( pet , ' Sleeps In The Sun' )
```

3 Save the file as "dog.py" so the module is named "dog"

4 Start a new program with a statement to make individual "dog" module functions available
```
from dog import bark , lick , nap
```

Next, call each function without supplying an argument
```
bark()
lick()
nap()
```

6 Now, call each function again and pass an argument value to each then save the file
```
bark( 'Pooch' )
lick( 'Pooch' )
nap( 'Pooch' )
```

7 Start another program by making all "dog" module functions available
```
from dog import *
```

fido.py

8 Request a user entry to overwrite the default parameter
```
pet = input( 'Enter A Pet Name: ' )
```

 Finally, call each function passing the user-defined value as the argument
```
bark( pet )
lick( pet )
nap( pet )
```

10 Save then run these programs – to see output from the imported functions

```
 ___                    Python Shell              - □ ×
File  Edit  Shell  Debug  Options  Windows  Help
>>> ============= RESTART ============ ====
>>>
A Dog Says WOOF!
A Dog Drinks Water
A Dog Sleeps In The Sun
Pooch Says WOOF!
Pooch Drinks Water
Pooch Sleeps In The Sun
>>> ============= RESTART ============ ====
>>>
Enter A Pet Name: Fido
Fido Says WOOF!
Fido Drinks Water
Fido Sleeps In The Sun
>>> |
```

Hot tip

For larger programs you can import modules into other modules to build a module hierarchy.

Summary

- Functions are defined using the **def** keyword followed by a name of your choice and **()** parentheses
- A function definition line must end with a : colon character and its block of statements to execute when the function gets called must be indented below that line
- Variables with global scope can be referenced from anywhere within that program
- Variables with local scope can only be referenced from within the function in which they are declared
- A local variable can be coerced to make it globally accessible by first declaring it using the **global** keyword
- Function parameters are special variables for use only within a function, and arguments are data values passed to parameters
- Parameters are declared as a comma-separated list within the parentheses of a function definition
- Function calls must supply argument data for each function parameter unless a default value is specified in their declaration
- Data passed to parameters in a function call must appear in the same order as the parameters unless their names are specified
- Optionally, the **return** keyword can be used within a function to return a value to the caller
- Functions can be stored in modules that are named as the file name without the ".py" file extension
- An **import** statement makes module functions available in a program by dot-suffixing their name after the module name
- Internally, each Python module has its own symbol table so like-named functions in different modules do not conflict
- A **from import** statement makes module functions available in a program without the need to dot-suffix their name
- An **import** * statement can be used to import a module's functions into the program's own symbol table

7 Sorting algorithms

This chapter demonstrates how to code a variety of sorting algorithm instruction sequences.

Copying sorts

An "algorithm" is a well-defined sequence of instructions to perform a specific task. Each algorithm takes one or more values as input and produces one or more resulting values as output.

An algorithm may be created in code as a function whose statements define a sequence of instructions to perform the task. Input values can be passed as arguments in the function call and resulting values can be returned as output from the function. Algorithms can be coded, using data structures and control structures in a variety of ways, to perform tasks such as sorting lists into order.

Sorting efficiency may depend upon the nature of the list to be sorted so different algorithms may be best-suited to particular tasks. Where the task requires a list to be sorted, while the original unsorted list remains intact, an algorithm function can be passed a reference to the list in an argument as input. The function can then make a copy of the original list, sort elements of that copy into order, then return the sorted copy list as output. This algorithm simply copies element values from the original list into a new list array then arranges them in ascending value order.

Python provides the **sort()** method for lists (described on page 52) but examples in this chapter demonstrate how to code various sorting algorithms that are found in many programming languages.

Array list elements are numbered from zero. So here, element [0] contains 5, element [1] contains 3, and so on.

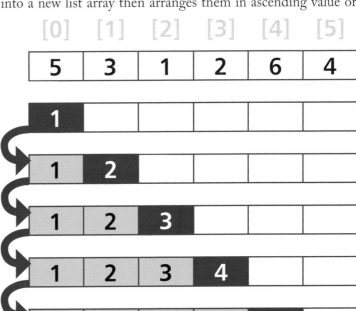

Start a new program by declaring a function to receive a list reference as input and return a sorted copy as output

```python
def copy_sort( array ) :
    copy = array[ : ]
    sorted_copy = [ ]
    # Algorithm sequence to be added here.
    return sorted_copy
```

copy.py

2 Next, add the indented algorithm sequence to insert the copied element values into the empty list in order

```python
while len( copy ) > 0 :
    minimum = 0
    for element in range( 0 , len( copy ) ) :
        if copy[ element ] < copy[ minimum ] :
            minimum = element
    print( '\tRemoving value' , copy[ minimum ] , \
            'from' , copy )
    sorted_copy.append( copy.pop( minimum ) )
```

Now, add statements to create and display an unsorted list

```python
array = [ 5 , 3 , 1 , 2 , 6 , 4 ]
print( 'Copy Sort...\nArray :' , array )
```

4 Finally, add statements to display the unsorted list and its sorted copy then save and run the program – to see the original list remains intact in unsorted order

```python
print( 'Copy :' , copy_sort( array ) )
print( 'Array :' , array )
```

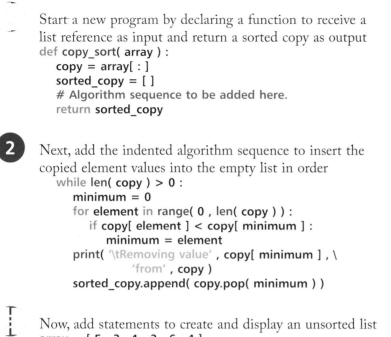

```
Python Shell                                    –  □  ×

File  Edit  Shell  Debug  Options  Windows  Help

>>> ============= RESTART ============= 
>>>
Copy Sort...
Array : [5, 3, 1, 2, 6, 4]
         Removing value 1 from [5, 3, 1, 2, 6, 4]
         Removing value 2 from [5, 3, 2, 6, 4]
         Removing value 3 from [5, 3, 6, 4]
         Removing value 4 from [5, 6, 4]
         Removing value 5 from [5, 6]
         Removing value 6 from [6]
Copy : [1, 2, 3, 4, 5, 6]
Array : [5, 3, 1, 2, 6, 4]
>>>|
```

Hot tip

Each value is popped off the list copy in sequence – to build the sorted version by appending each to the empty array.

Selecting sorts

Often you will want to sort the elements of an unsorted list array "in place" rather than sort a copy of the original list, as demonstrated in the previous example. There are several popular algorithms you can employ to sort arrays in place, each using a different technique with their own strengths and weaknesses.

A "selection sort" algorithm examines each element in the unsorted part of an array list and selects the element containing the lowest value. It then swaps the selected element value with that contained in the element at the beginning of the unsorted part of the array list – thereby increasing the size of the sorted part of the array and decreasing its unsorted part. This process is repeated until all element values are sorted into ascending order.

Selection sort is a simple swap-based algorithm that is relatively easy to understand and code as a function algorithm. It is one of the two most efficient algorithms for sorting small arrays of 20 or so elements.

In this example, the final element will already contain the highest value when the penultimate element has been sorted.

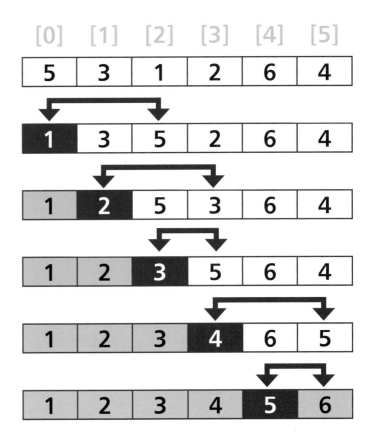

1 Start a new program by declaring a function to receive a list reference as input and begin a loop to store each element's value and current index number

selection.py

```python
def selection_sort( array ) :

    for index in range( 0 , len( array ) -1 ) :
        value = array[ index ]
        current = index

        # Algorithm sequence to be added here.
```

2 Next, add the algorithm sequence to repeatedly swap the smallest unsorted value with the first unsorted value

```python
        for element in range( index+1 , len( array ) ) :
            if array[ element ] < array[ current ] :
                current = element
        array[ index ] = array[ current ]
        array[ current ]= value

        print( '\tResolving element[' , index , '] to ' , array )
```

3 Now, add statements to create and display an unsorted list

```python
array = [ 5 , 3 , 1 , 2 , 6 , 4 ]
print( 'Selection Sort...\nArray :' , array )
```

4 Finally, add statements to call the algorithm function and display the list once more – to see the list sorted in place

```python
selection_sort( array )
print( 'Array :' , array )
```

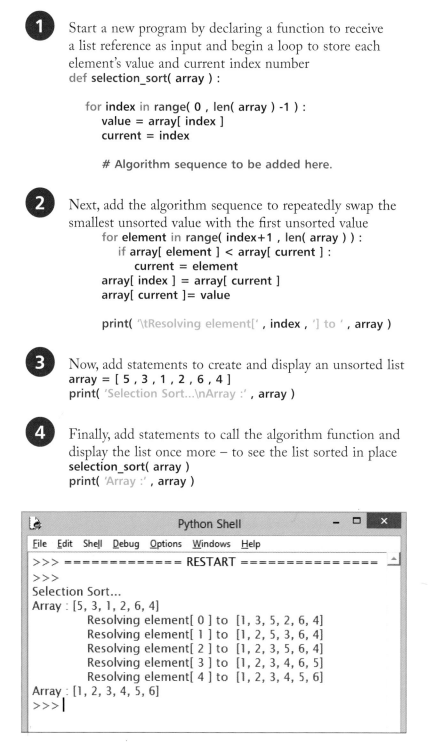

```
┌─────────────────────────────────────────────────┐
│  ⌨              Python Shell           – □  ✕     │
├─────────────────────────────────────────────────┤
│ File  Edit  Shell  Debug  Options  Windows  Help │
│ >>> ============ RESTART ================        │
│ >>>                                              │
│ Selection Sort...                                │
│ Array : [5, 3, 1, 2, 6, 4]                       │
│         Resolving element[ 0 ] to [1, 3, 5, 2, 6, 4] │
│         Resolving element[ 1 ] to [1, 2, 5, 3, 6, 4] │
│         Resolving element[ 2 ] to [1, 2, 3, 5, 6, 4] │
│         Resolving element[ 3 ] to [1, 2, 3, 4, 6, 5] │
│         Resolving element[ 4 ] to [1, 2, 3, 4, 5, 6] │
│ Array : [1, 2, 3, 4, 5, 6]                       │
│ >>> |                                            │
└─────────────────────────────────────────────────┘
```

Don't forget

Sorting in place swaps the element values contained in the original referenced array list.

Inserting sorts

The technique of swapping elements with a selection sort algorithm, demonstrated in the previous example, works well but an alternative technique can be employed to simply insert elements into an array list at the correct ascending order position.

An "insertion sort" algorithm examines the next element in the unsorted part of an array list and, if required, inserts the element at the correct ascending order position in the array list. To accommodate the inserted element, all other elements in the unsorted part of the list shift to the right – increasing the size of the sorted part of the array and decreasing its unsorted part. This process is repeated for each element in turn until all element values are sorted into ascending order.

Insertion sort is a simple algorithm that is relatively easy to understand and code as a function algorithm. Along with the selection sort algorithm it is one of the two most efficient algorithms for sorting small arrays of 20 or so elements. Typically, insertion sort will require fewer comparisons than a selection sort so is often seen as the best method for sorting small arrays.

In this example, two steps are needed to get the lowest value into the very first element – as 3 is less than 5, then 1 is less than 3.

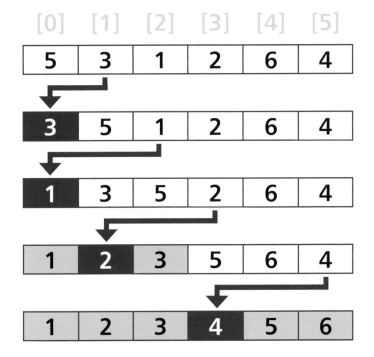

Start a new program by declaring a function to receive a list reference as input and begin a loop to store the current element's value

```python
def insertion_sort( array ) :

    for index in range( 1 , len( array ) ) :
        value = array[ index ]

        # Algorithm sequence to be added here.

        print( '\tResolving element[' , index , '] to ' , array )
```

insertion.py

2 Next, add the algorithm sequence to repeatedly insert the current value if smaller than that in the current element

```python
        while array[ index-1 ] > value and index >= 1 :
            array[ index ] = array[ index-1 ]
            index -=1
            array[ index ] = value
```

Now, add statements to create and display an unsorted list

```python
array = [ 5 , 3 , 1 , 2 , 6 , 4 ]
print( 'Insertion Sort...\nArray :' , array )
```

4 Finally, add statements to call the algorithm function and display the list once more – to see the list sorted in place

```python
insertion_sort( array )
print( 'Array :' , array )
```

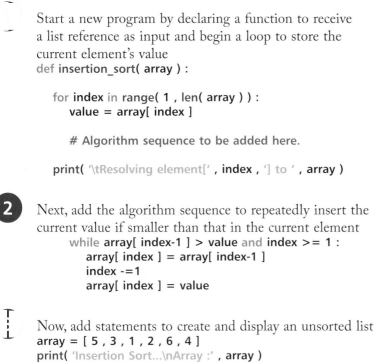

```
                        Python Shell              –  □  ×
File  Edit  Shell  Debug  Options  Windows  Help
>>> ============= RESTART ================
>>>
Insertion Sort...
Array : [5, 3, 1, 2, 6, 4]
            Resolving element[ 0 ] to [3, 5, 1, 2, 6, 4]
            Resolving element[ 0 ] to [1, 3, 5, 2, 6, 4]
            Resolving element[ 1 ] to [1, 2, 3, 5, 6, 4]
            Resolving element[ 4 ] to [1, 2, 3, 5, 6, 4]
            Resolving element[ 3 ] to [1, 2, 3, 4, 5, 6]
Array : [1, 2, 3, 4, 5, 6]
>>> |
```

Hot tip

On some iterations this algorithm recognizes that elements in the "unsorted" part are already sorted following earlier insertions.

Bubbling sorts

A "bubble sort" algorithm is a further simple alternative to the selection and insertion sort techniques. This algorithm repeatedly examines each adjacent pair of elements in an array list and, if required, swaps them around to place a lower value before a higher value – until all elements are sorted into ascending order.

Bubble sort is a simple algorithm that is very easy to understand and code as a function algorithm. Although the bubble sort technique is generally less efficient than insertion sort or selection sort, it is one of the quickest algorithms for nearly-sorted arrays.

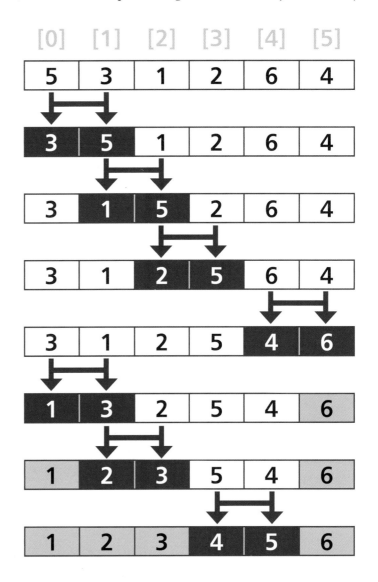

Don't forget

In this example, no swap is needed on the first pass for element [3] and [4] as their values 5 and 6 are in correct order.

1 Start a new program by declaring a function to receive a list reference as input and begin an outer loop to repeatedly iterate through the array list

```python
def bubble_sort( array ) :

    for index in range( len( array ) ) :

    # Algorithm sequence to be added here.
```

bubble.py

2 Next, add the algorithm sequence to iterate through the array list elements, up to the penultimate element, and swap values if the next is greater than the current value

```python
        for element in range( len( array -1 ) - index ) :
            if array[ element ] > array[ element+1 ] :
                array[ element ] , array[ element+1 ] = \
                    array[ element+1 ] , array[ element ]

            print( '\tResolving element[' , element , \
                '] to ' , array )
```

3 Now, add statements to create and display an unsorted list

```python
array = [ 5 , 3 , 1 , 2 , 6 , 4 ]
print( 'Bubble Sort...\nArray :' , array )
```

4 Finally, add statements to call the algorithm function and display the list once more – to see the list sorted in place

```python
bubble_sort( array )
print( 'Array :' , array )
```

```
┌─────────────────────────────────────────────────┐
│ ⌨              Python Shell           – □ ✕      │
├─────────────────────────────────────────────────┤
│ File  Edit  Shell  Debug  Options  Windows  Help │
│ >>> ============== RESTART ================ ▲    │
│ >>>                                              │
│ Bubble Sort...                                   │
│ Array : [5, 3, 1, 2, 6, 4]                       │
│          Resolving element[ 0 ] to [3, 5, 1, 2, 6, 4] │
│          Resolving element[ 1 ] to [3, 1, 5, 2, 6, 4] │
│          Resolving element[ 2 ] to [3, 1, 2, 5, 6, 4] │
│          Resolving element[ 4 ] to [3, 1, 2, 5, 4, 6] │
│          Resolving element[ 0 ] to [1, 3, 2, 5, 4, 6] │
│          Resolving element[ 1 ] to [1, 2, 3, 5, 4, 6] │
│          Resolving element[ 3 ] to [1, 2, 3, 4, 5, 6] │
│ Array : [1, 2, 3, 4, 5, 6]                       │
│ >>>|                                             │
└─────────────────────────────────────────────────┘
```

Hot tip

In average simple cases, insertion sort outperforms selection sort, and selection sort outperforms bubble sort.

Merging sorts

While the simple selection sort, insertion sort, and bubble sort techniques work well on small array lists, more efficient complex sorting algorithms generally work better on larger array lists. Typically, these complex sorting algorithms employ a "divide and conquer" strategy to first repeatedly divide the list into sub-sections, then re-assemble those sub-sections in sorted order.

A "merge sort" algorithm is a complex sorting algorithm that first repeatedly divides an array into left and right sub-sections from the array's mid-point until it is empty or has just one element. Once the division is complete, all sub-sections are individual elements. The algorithm then merges all the individual elements into a single sorted list.

Merge sort is a complex algorithm that can be coded as a function algorithm, which makes "recursive" calls to repeatedly divide an array. Merge sort is a fast algorithm that only compares element values when merging the elements back into a sorted array list.

In this example, the array is only small but the merge sort algorithm efficiently divides then re-assembles large arrays in exactly the same way.

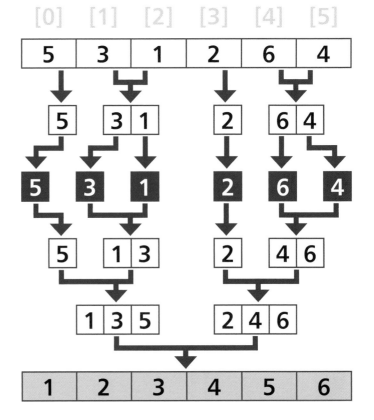

...cont'd

1 Start a new program by declaring a function to receive a list reference and repeatedly iterate through an array list

```python
def merge_sort( array ) :
    if len( array ) > 1 :
        middle = int( len( array ) / 2 )
        left = array[ 0 : middle ]  ;  right = array[ middle : ]
        print( '\tSplit to' , left , right )
        merge_sort( left )  ;  merge_sort( right )
        # Algorithm sequence to be added here.
```

merge.py

2 Next, add the algorithm sequence to divide the array list elements into sub-sections then merge them together

```python
        i = j = 0
        for element in range( len( array ) ) :
            L = left[ i ] if i < len( left ) else None
            R = right[ j ] if j < len( right ) else None
            if( ( L and R ) and ( L < R ) ) or R is None :
                array[ element ] = L  ;  i += 1
            elif( ( L and R ) and ( L >= R ) ) or L is None :
                array[ element ] = R  ;  j += 1
        print( '\t\tMerging' , left , right )
```

3 Now, add statements to create and display the array list

```python
array = [ 5 , 3 , 1 , 2 , 6 , 4 ]
print( 'Merge Sort...\nArray :' , array )
merge_sort( array )
print( 'Array :' , array )
```

```
Python Shell                              – □ ×
File  Edit  Shell  Debug  Options  Windows  Help
>>> ============= RESTART =============
>>>
Merge Sort...
Array : [5, 3, 1, 2, 6, 4]
        Split to [5, 3, 1] [2, 6, 4]
        Split to [5] [3, 1]
        Split to [3] [1]
                Merging [3] [1]
                Merging [5] [1, 3]
        Split to [2] [6, 4]
        Split to [6] [4]
                Merging [6] [4]
                Merging [2] [4, 6]
                Merging [1, 3, 5] [2, 4, 6]
Array : [1, 2, 3, 4, 5, 6]
>>>
```

Hot tip

The code listed here uses a semi-colon ; separator to write two statements on some lines – due only to page limitations.

Partitioning sorts

The technique of dividing an array list into sub-sections around the array's mid-point with a merge sort algorithm, demonstrated in the previous example, works well but an alternative technique can be employed to partition an array list around a "pivot" point.

A "quick sort" algorithm is a complex sorting algorithm that also employs the "divide and conquer" strategy. This first specifies a particular array element whose value will act as the pivot. The algorithm then repeatedly divides the array into two "partitions" – one partition containing values less than the pivot and the other partition containing values more than the pivot. Once the partition operation is complete, the final pivot is in its correct position so the algorithm then merges the lesser partition with the pivot and the greater partition into a single sorted list.

Quick sort is a complex algorithm that can be coded as a function algorithm, which makes "recursive" calls to repeatedly divide an array. Quick sort is a fast algorithm that compares element values when dividing the elements into partitions.

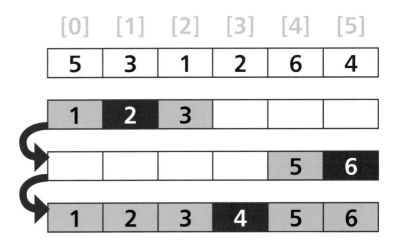

In this example the array is only small but the quick sort algorithm efficiently partitions then re-assembles large arrays in exactly the same way.

Opinions vary as to which element is best to choose as the pivot in the quick sort algorithm. Some coders like to choose a middle element, as in the merge sort algorithm in the previous example. Others prefer to choose the first or last element, or an element at some arbitrary position in between – like the example opposite.

...cont'd

1 Start a new program by declaring a function to receive a list reference and repeatedly iterate through an array list

```
def quick_sort( array ) :
    if len( array ) > 1 :
        pivot = int( len( array ) -1 )
        less = [ ] ; more = [ ]
        # Algorithm sequence to be added here.
        quick_sort( less ) ; quick_sort( more )
        print( '\tLess:' , less , '\tPivot:' , array[ pivot ] , \
            '\tMore:' , more )
        array[ : ] = less + [ array[ pivot ] ] + more
        print( '\t\t...Merged:' , array )
```

quick.py

2 Next, add the algorithm sequence to divide the array list elements into partitions then merge them together

```
for element in range( len( array ) ) :
    value = array[ element ]
    if element != pivot :
        if value < array[ pivot ] :
            less.append( value )
        else :
            more.append( value )
```

3 Now, add statements to create and display the array list

```
array = [ 5 , 3 , 1 , 2 , 6 , 4 ]
print( 'Quick Sort...\nArray :' , array )
quick_sort( array )
print( 'Array :' , array )
```

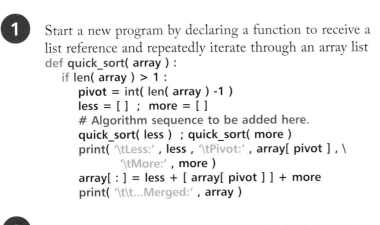

```
>>> ============== RESTART ==============
>>>
Quick Sort...
Array : [5, 3, 1, 2, 6, 4]
            Less: [1]  Pivot: 2   More: [3]
                    ...Merged: [1, 2, 3]
            Less: [5]  Pivot: 6   More: []
                    ...Merged: [5, 6]
            Less: [1, 2, 3]      Pivot: 4   More: [5, 6]
                    ...Merged: [1, 2, 3, 4, 5, 6]
Array : [1, 2, 3, 4, 5, 6]
>>> |
```

The quick sort algorithm uses less memory than merge sort and is often considered to be the best sorting algorithm.

Summary

- An algorithm is a well-defined sequence of instructions to perform a specific task

- Each algorithm takes one or more values as input and produces one or more resulting values as output

- An algorithm may be created in code as a function whose statements define a sequence of instructions to perform a task

- The efficiency of sorting algorithms may depend upon the nature of the list to be sorted

- A sorting algorithm function can make a copy of a list passed as input and return a sorted copy of that list as output

- There are several popular algorithms to sort array lists in place but each have their own strengths and weaknesses

- Selection Sort algorithms repeatedly select the lowest element in the unsorted section of an array list and move it to the end of the sorted section of that array

- Insertion Sort algorithms repeatedly take the next element in the unsorted section of an array list and insert it into the sorted section of that array at the correct position

- Bubble Sort algorithms repeatedly compare adjacent elements in an unsorted array list and swap them into the correct order

- Selection Sort, Insertion Sort, and Bubble Sort are simple comparison algorithms but are relatively slow

- Merge Sort algorithms repeatedly divide an unsorted array list into left and right sub-sections from the array's mid-point then merge the sub-sections into a single sorted list

- Quick Sort algorithms repeatedly divide an unsorted array list into partitions containing values greater or less than a pivot value then merge the partitions into a single sorted list

- Merge Sort and Quick Sort algorithms are fast complex algorithms that each employ a divide-and-conquer strategy

8

Importing libraries

This chapter demonstrates how to code pre-defined library functionality into your programs.

Inspecting Python

Python includes "sys" and "keyword" modules that are useful for interrogating the Python system itself. The keyword module contains a list of all Python keywords in its **kwlist** attribute and provides an **iskeyword()** function if you want to test any word.

You can explore the many features of the "sys" module and indeed any feature of Python using the Interactive Mode help system. Just type **help()** at the **>>>** prompt to start the Help system, then type **sys** at the **help>** prompt that appears.

Perhaps, most usefully, the "sys" module has attributes that contain the Python version number, interpreter location on your system, and a list of all directories where the interpreter seeks module files – so if you save module files in any of these directories you can be sure the interpreter will find them.

system.py

1 Start a new program by importing the "sys" and "keyword" modules to make their features available
import **sys** , **keyword**

2 Next, add a statement to display the Python version
print('Python Version:' , **sys.version**)

3 Now, add a statement to display the actual location on your system of the Python interpreter
print('Python Interpreter Location:' , **sys.executable**)

4 Then, add statements to display a list of all directories where the Python interpreter looks for module files
print('Python Module Search Path: ')
for **folder** in **sys.path** :
        print(folder)

5 Finally, add statements to display a list all the Python keywords
print('Python Keywords: ')
for **word** in **keyword.kwlist** :
        print(word)

6 Save and then run the program – to see details of the Python version on your own system

The first item on the Python search path is your current directory – so any file within there or within any subdirectories you make there will be found by the Python interpreter.

Spend a little time with the Interactive Mode help utility to discover lots more about Python.

Doing mathematics

Python includes a "math" module that provides lots of functions you can use to perform mathematical procedures once imported.

The **math.ceil()** and **math.floor()** functions enable a program to perform rounding of a floating point value specified between their parentheses to the closest integer – **math.ceil()** rounds up and **math.floor()** rounds down but the value returned, although an integer, is a **float** data type rather than an **int** data type.

The **math.pow()** function requires two arguments to raise a specified value by a specified power. The **math.sqrt()** function, on the other hand, simply requires a single argument and returns the square root of that specified value. Both function results are returned as a numeric value of the **float** data type.

Typical trigonometry can be performed using functions from the math module too, such as **math.sin()**, **math.cosin()** and **math.tan()**.

Additionally, Python includes a "random" module that can be used to produce pseudo random numbers once imported into a program.

The **random.random()** function produces a single floating-point number between zero and 1.0. Perhaps, more interestingly, the **random.sample()** function produces a list of elements selected at random from a sequence. This method requires two arguments to specify the sequence to select from, and the length of the list to be produced. As the **range()** function returns a sequence of numbers, this can be used to specify a sequence as the first argument to the **random.sample()** function – so it will randomly select numbers from that sequence to produce a list in which no numbers repeat.

Integers can be cast from the **int** data type to the **float** data type using the **float()** function and to the **string** data type using the **str()** function.

maths.py

1 Start a new program by importing the "math" and "random" modules to make their features available
`import math , random`

2 Next, add statements to display two rounded values
`print( 'Rounded Up 9.5:' , math.ceil( 9.5 ) )`
`print( 'Rounded Down 9.5:' , math.floor( 9.5 ) )`

3 Now, add a statement to initialize a variable with an integer value
`num = 4`

...cont'd

4 Add statements to display the square and square root of the variable value
```python
print( num , 'Squared:' , math.pow( num , 2 ) )
print( num , 'Square Root:' , math.sqrt( num ) )
```

5 Then, add a statement to produce a random list of six unique numbers between one and 49
```python
nums = random.sample( range( 1, 49 ) , 6 )
```

6 Finally, add a statement to display the random list
```python
print( 'Your Lucky Lotto Numbers Are:' , nums )
```

7 Save then run the program – to see math results and random samples

Don't forget

All the math functions here return floating-point numbers of the **float** data type.

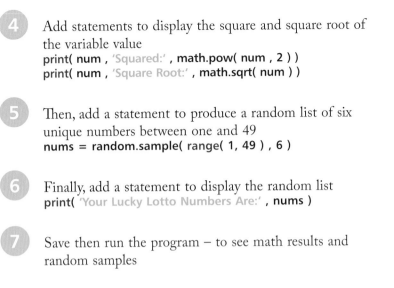
```
                    Python Shell           –  □  ×
File  Edit  Shell  Debug  Options  Windows  Help
>>> ============= RESTART =============
>>>
Rounded Up 9.5: 10
Rounded Down 9.5: 9
4 Squared: 16.0
4 Square Root: 2.0
Your Lucky Lotto Numbers Are: [23, 4, 5, 29, 1, 8]
>>> ============= RESTART =============
>>>
Rounded Up 9.5: 10
Rounded Down 9.5: 9
4 Squared: 16.0
4 Square Root: 2.0
Your Lucky Lotto Numbers Are: [12, 31, 40, 36, 15, 41]
>>> ============= RESTART =============
>>>
Rounded Up 9.5: 10
Rounded Down 9.5: 9
4 Squared: 16.0
4 Square Root: 2.0
Your Lucky Lotto Numbers Are: [43, 39, 1, 25, 35, 30]
>>> ============= RESTART =============
>>>
Rounded Up 9.5: 10
Rounded Down 9.5: 9
4 Squared: 16.0
4 Square Root: 2.0
Your Lucky Lotto Numbers Are: [8, 2, 33, 42, 45, 6]
>>>|
```

Hot tip

The list produced by **random.sample()** does not actually replace elements of the sequence but merely copies a sample, as its name says.

Calculating decimals

Python programs that attempt floating-point arithmetic can produce unexpected and inaccurate results because the floating-point numbers cannot accurately represent all decimal numbers.

inaccurate.py

1   Start a new program by initializing two variables with floating-point values
```
item = 0.70
rate = 1.05
```

2   Next, initialize two more variables by attempting floating-point arithmetic with the first two variables
```
tax = item * rate
total = item + tax
```

3   Now, add statements to display variable values formatted to have two decimal places so trailing zeros are shown
```
print( 'Item:\t' , '%.2f' % item )
print( 'Tax:\t' , '%.2f' % tax )
print( 'Total:\t' , '%.2f' % total )
```

Hot tip

Here, the variable values are formatted using a string substitution technique to show two decimal places – described in more detail on page 114.

4   Save then run the program – to see the output display an inaccurate addition total

```
Python Shell                                    _  □  ×
File  Edit  Shell  Debug  Options  Windows  Help
>>> ============= RESTART ==============
>>>
Item:      0.70
Tax:       0.73
Total:     1.44
>>> |
```

5   To help understand this problem edit all three print statements to display the variable values expanded to <u>20</u> decimal places, then run the modified program
```
print( 'Item:\t' , '%.20f' % item )
print( 'Tax:\t' , '%.20f' % tax )
print( 'Total:\t' , '%.20f' % total )
```

expanded.py

```
Python Shell                    – □ ✕
File  Edit  Shell  Debug  Options  Windows  Help
>>> ============= RESTART ==============
>>>
Item:     0.6999999999999995559
Tax:      0.7349999999999998668
Total:    1.4350000000000005329
>>>|
```

This problem is not unique to Python – Java has a BigDecimal class that overcomes this problem in much the same way as the decimal module in Python.

It is now clear that the tax value is represented numerically slightly below 0.735 so gets rounded down to 0.73. Conversely, the total value is represented numerically slightly above 1.435 so gets rounded up to 1.44, creating the apparent addition error.

Errors in floating-point arithmetic can be avoided using Python's "decimal" module. This provides a **Decimal()** object with which floating-point numbers can be more accurately represented.

6 Add a statement at the beginning of the program to import the "decimal" module to make all features available
   from **decimal** import *

decimals.py

7 Next, edit the first two variable assignment to objects
   item = Decimal(0.70)
   rate = Decimal(1.05)

8 Save the changes then run the modified program to see both tax and total representations will now get rounded down – so the output will show accurate addition when string formatting is changed back to two decimal places

Always use the **Decimal()** object to calculate monetary values or anywhere that accuracy is essential.

```
Python Shell                    – □ ✕
File  Edit  Shell  Debug  Options  Windows  Help
>>> ============= RESTART ==============
>>>
Item:     0.70
Tax:      0.73
Total:    1.43
>>>|
```

Telling time

The Python "datetime" module can be imported into a program to make use of times and dates. It provides a **datetime** object with attributes of **year, month, day, hour, minute, second, microsecond**.

A **datetime** object has a **today()** function that assigns the current date and time values to its attributes and returns them in a tuple. It also has a **getattr()** function that requires two arguments specifying the datetime object name and attribute to retrieve. Alternatively, the attributes can be referenced using dot notation such as **datetime.year**.

All values in a **datetime** object are stored as numeric values but can be usefully transformed into text equivalents using its **strftime()** function. This requires a single string argument that is a "directive" specifying which part of the tuple to return and in what format. The possible directives are listed in the table below:

Hot tip

As the datetime object is in a module of the same name, simply importing the module means it would be referenced as **datetime.datetime**. Use **from datetime import *** so it can be referenced just as **datetime** alone.

Beware

As the **strftime()** function requires a string argument, the directive must be enclosed between quote marks.

Directive:	Returns:
%A	Full weekday name (%a for abbreviated day name)
%B	Full month name (%b for abbreviated month name)
%c	Date and time appropriate for locale
%d	Day of the month number 1-31
%f	Microsecond number 0-999999
%H	Hour number 0-23 (24-hour clock)
%I	Hour number 1-12 (12-hour clock)
%j	Day of the year number 0-366
%m	Month number 1-12
%M	Minute number 0-59
%p	AM or PM equivalent for locale
%S	Second number 0-59
%w	Week day number 0(Sunday)-6
%W	Week of the year number 0-53
%X	Time appropriate for locale (%x for appropriate date)
%Y	Year 0001-9999 (%y for year 00-99)
%z	Timezone offset from UTC as +HHMM or -HHMM
%Z	Timezone name

...cont'd

1 Start a new program by importing the "datetime" module to make its features available
```
from datetime import *
```

time.py

2 Next, create a datetime object with attributes assigned current date and time values then display its contents
```
today = datetime.today()
print( 'Today Is:' , today )
```

3 Add a loop to display each attribute value individually
```
for attr in \
[ 'year','month','day','hour','minute','second','microsecond' ] :
        print( attr , ':\t' , getattr( today , attr ) )
```

4 Now, add a statement to display time using dot notation
```
print( ' Time:' , today.hour , ':' , today.minute , sep = '' )
```

Hot tip

Notice how the \ backslash character is used in this loop to allow a statement to continue on the next line without causing an error.

5 Then, assign formatted day and month names to variables
```
day = today.strftime( '%A' )
month = today.strftime( '%B' )
```

6 Finally, add a statement to display the formatted date
```
print( 'Date:' , day , month , today.day )
```

7 Save then run the program – to see the date and time values get displayed

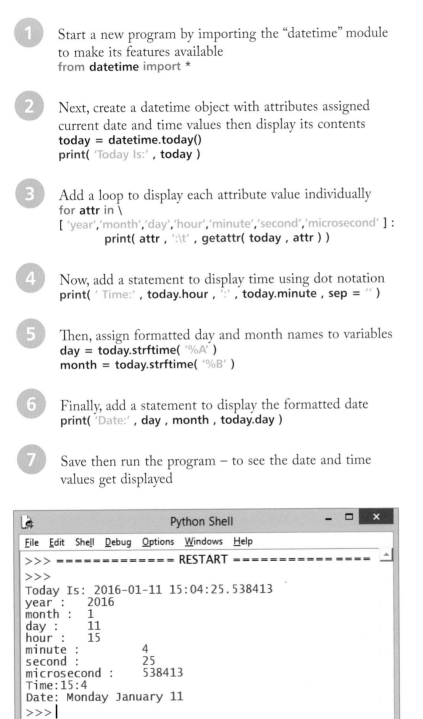

```
                    Python Shell                    ─ □ ×
File  Edit  Shell  Debug  Options  Windows  Help
>>> ============== RESTART =================
>>>
Today Is: 2016-01-11 15:04:25.538413
year :    2016
month :   1
day :     11
hour :    15
minute :          4
second :          25
microsecond :     538413
Time:15:4
Date: Monday January 11
>>> |
```

Hot tip

You can assign new values to attributes of a datetime object using its **replace()** function, such as **today = today.replace(year=2016)**

Running timers

Getting the current time both before and after an event means that the duration of the event can be calculated by their difference. The Python "time" module can be imported into a program to provide various time-related functions.

Current system time is usually counted as the number of seconds elapsed since the Epoch at 00:00:00 GMT on January 1, 1970. The **time** module's **time()** function returns the current time in seconds since the Epoch as a floating point number when called.

The figure returned by the **time()** function can be converted into a "struct_time" object using **gmtime()** or **localtime()** functions. This object has attributes of **tm_year, tm_mon, tm_mday, tm_hour, tm_min, tm_sec, tm_wday, tm_yday, tm_yday** and **tm_isdst** that can be referenced using dot notation. For example, *struct*.**tm_wday**.

All values in a **struct_time** object are stored as numeric values but can be transformed into text equivalents using the **strftime()** function. This requires an argument that is a format "directive" followed by the name of the **struct_time** object. The possible directives include those listed in the table on page 106 for the **datetime** object. For example, **strftime(** '%A' , *struct* **)** for weekday.

Usefully, the **time** module also provides a **sleep()** function that can be used to pause execution of a program. Its argument specifies the amount of time in seconds by which to delay execution.

timer.py

1 Start a new program by importing the "time" module to make its features available
   from time import *

2 Next, initialize a variable with a floating point number that is the current elapsed time since the epoch
   start_timer = time()

3 Now, add a statement to create a **struct_time** object from the elapsed time value
   struct = localtime(start_timer)

4 Then, announce that a countdown timer is about to begin from the current time starting point
   print('Starting Countdown At:' , **strftime(** '%X' , **struct))**

5 Add a loop to initialize and print a counter variable value then decrement the counter by one and pause for one second on each iteration

```
i = 10
while i > -1 :
        print( i )
        i -= 1
        sleep( 1 )
```

6 Next, initialize a variable with a floating point number that is the current elapsed time now since the Epoch

```
end_timer = time()
```

7 Now, initialize a variable with the rounded seconds value of the time difference between the two timed points

```
difference = round( end_timer - start_timer )
```

8 Finally, add a statement to display the time taken to execute the countdown loop

```
print( '\nRuntime:' , difference , 'Seconds' )
```

9 Save then run the program – to see the loop pause on each iteration and elapsed time

Hot tip

The argument to the **sleep()** function may be a floating point number to indicate a more precise sleep pause time.

```
Python Shell                                    –  □  ×
File  Edit  Shell  Debug  Options  Windows  Help
>>> ============= RESTART ================
>>>
Starting Countdown At: 10:36:08
10
9
8
7
6
5
4
3
2
1
0

Runtime: 11 Seconds
>>>
```

Beware

Do not confuse the **time.strftime()** function used in this example with the **datetime.strftime()** function used in the previous example.

Summary

- The **sys** module has attributes that contain the Python version number, interpreter location, and path to search for modules

- The **keyword** module has a **kwlist** attribute that contains a list of all current Python keywords

- The **math** module provides functions to perform mathematical procedures such as **math.ceil()** and **math.floor()**

- The **math.pow()** and **math.sqrt()** functions both return their results as a decimal value of the **float** data type

- Trigonometry can be performed using **math** module functions such as **math.sin()**, **math.cosin()** and **math.tan()**

- The **random** module provides a **random()** function that produces pseudo random numbers and a **sample()** function that produces a list of elements selected at random from a sequence

- Floating-point **float** numbers cannot accurately represent all decimal numbers

- The **decimal** module provides a **Decimal()** object with which floating-point numbers can be accurately represented to calculate monetary values

- The **datetime** module provides a **datetime** object with **year, month, day, hour, minute, second, microsecond** attributes that can be referenced by dot-suffixing or with the **getattr()** function

- A **datetime** object has a **strftime()** function that can specify a directive to return a formatted part of the object

- The **time** module provides a **time()** function that returns the current elapsed time in seconds since the Epoch

- The **gmtime()** and **localtime()** functions return a **struct_time** object with attributes containing date and time components

9 Managing text

This chapter demonstrates how to manipulate text strings in your programs and how to store text in files.

Manipulating strings

String values can be manipulated in a Python program using the various operators listed in the table below:

Operator:	Description:	Example:
+	Concatenate – join strings together	'Hello' + 'Mike'
*	Repeat – multiply the string	'Hello' * 2
[ ]	Slice – select a character at a specified index position	'Hello' [0]
[:]	Range Slice – select characters in a specified index range	'Hello' [0 : 4]
in	Membership Inclusive – return True if character exists in the string	'H' in 'Hello'
not in	Membership Exclusive – return True if character doesn't exist in string	'h' not in 'Hello'
r/R	Raw String – suppress meaning of escape characters	print(r'\n')
''' '''	Docstring – describe a module, function, class, or method	def sum(a,b) : ''' Add Args '''

The [ ] slice operator and [:] range slice operator recognize that a string is simply a list containing an individual character within each list element, which can be referenced by their index number.

Similarly, the **in** and **not in** membership operators iterate through each element seeking to match the specified character.

The raw string operator **r** (or uppercase **R**) must be placed immediately before the opening quote mark to suppress escape characters in the string and is useful when the string contains the backslash character.

A "docstring" is a descriptive string literal that occurs as the first statement in a module, a function, a class, or a method definition. This should be enclosed within triple single quote marks. Uniquely, the docstring becomes the **__doc__** special attribute of that object, so can be referenced using its name and dot-suffixing. All modules should normally have docstrings, and all functions and classes exported by a module should also have docstrings.

Beware

The membership operators perform a case-sensitive match, so **'A' in 'abc'** will fail.

Beware

The Range Slice returns the string up to, but not including, the final specified index position.

1 Start a new program by defining a simple function that includes a docstring description

```
def display( s ) :
    '''Display an argument value.'''
    print( s )
```

manipulate.py

2 Next, add a statement to display the function description

```
display( display.__doc__ )
```

3 Now, add a statement to display a raw string value that contains the backslash character

```
display( r'C:\Program Files' )
```

4 Then, add a statement to display a concatenation of two string values that include an escape character and a space

```
display( '\nHello' + ' Python' )
```

Remember that strings must be enclosed within either single quote marks or double quote marks.

5 Next, add a statement to display a slice of a specified string within a range of element index numbers

```
display( 'Python In Easy Steps\n' [ 7 : ] )
```

6 Finally, display the results of seeking characters within a specified string

```
display( 'P' in 'Python' )
display( 'p' in 'Python' )
```

7 Save then run the program – to see manipulated strings get displayed

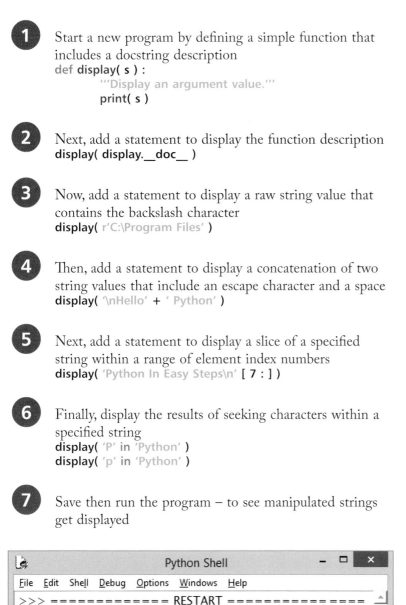

```
                   Python Shell              –  □  ×
File  Edit  Shell  Debug  Options  Windows  Help
>>> ============= RESTART ===============
>>>
Display an argument value.
C:\Program Files

Hello Python
In Easy Steps

True
False
>>>
```

With range slice, if the start index number is omitted zero is assumed and if the end index number is omitted the string length is assumed.

Formatting strings

The Python built-in **dir()** function can be useful to examine the names of functions and variables defined in a module by specifying the module name within its parentheses. Interactive mode can easily be used for this purpose by importing the module name then calling the **dir()** function. The example below examines the "dog" module created on page 82 in Chapter Six:

```
                                    Python Shell              —  ☐   ✕
 File  Edit  Shell  Debug  Options  Windows  Help
>>> import dog
>>> for i in dir( dog ) :
        print( i )
__builtins__
__cached__
__doc__
__file__
__loader__
__name__
__package__
__spec__
bark
lick
nap
>>> |
```

Those defined names that begin and end with a double underscore are Python objects, whereas the others are programmer-defined. The **__builtins__** module can also be examined using the **dir()** function, to reveal the names of functions and variables defined by default, such as the **print()** function and a **str** object.

The **str** object defines several useful functions for string formatting, including an actual **format()** function that performs replacements. A string to be formatted by the **format()** function can contain both text and "replacement fields" marking places where text is to be inserted from an ordered comma-separated list of values. Each replacement field is denoted by **{ }** braces, which may optionally contain the index number position of the replacement in the list.

Strings may also be formatted using the C-style **%s** substitution operator to mark places in a string where text is to be inserted from a comma-separated ordered list of values.

1 Start a new program by initializing a variable with a formatted string
snack = '{} and {}'.format('Burger' , 'Fries')

2 Next, display the variable value to see the text replaced in their listed order
print('\nReplaced:' , snack)

format.py

3 Now, assign a differently formatted string to the variable
snack = '{1} and {0}'.format('Burger' , 'Fries')

4 Then, display the variable value again to see the text now replaced by their specified index element value
print('Replaced:' , snack)

Beware

5 Assign another formatted string to the variable
snack = '%s and %s' % ('Milk' , 'Cookies')

You cannot leave spaces around the index number in the replacement field.

6 Finally, display the variable value once more to see the text substituted in their listed order
print('\nSubstituted:' , snack)

115

7 Save then run the program – to see formatted strings get displayed

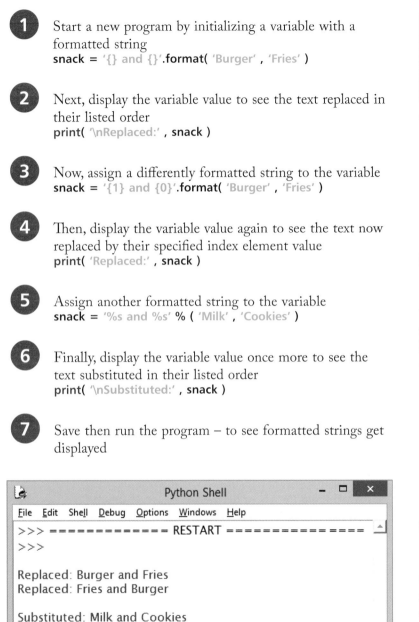

```
Python Shell                                    –  □  ×
File  Edit  Shell  Debug  Options  Windows  Help
>>> ============== RESTART ===============
>>>

Replaced: Burger and Fries
Replaced: Fries and Burger

Substituted: Milk and Cookies
>>>
```

Hot tip

Other data types can be substituted using **%d** for a decimal integer, **%c** for a character, and **%f** for a floating-point number.

Modifying strings

The Python **str** object has many useful functions that can be dot-suffixed to its name for modification of the string and to examine its contents. Most commonly used string modification functions are listed in the table below together with a brief description:

Method:	Description:
capitalize( )	Change string's first letter to uppercase
title( )	Change all first letters to uppercase
upper( ) lower( ) swapcase( )	Change the case of all letters to uppercase, to lowercase, or to the inverse of the current case respectively
join(*seq*)	Merge string into separator sequence *seq*
lstrip( ) rstrip ( ) strip( )	Remove leading whitespace, trailing whitespace, or both leading and trailing whitespace respectively
replace(*old* , *new*)	Replace all occurrences of *old* with *new*
ljust(*w* , *c*) rjust(*w* , *c*)	Pad string to right or left respectively to total column width *w* with character *c*
center(*w* , *c*)	Pad string each side to total column width *w* with character *c* (default is space)
count(*sub*)	Return the number of occurrences of *sub*
find(*sub*)	Return the index number of the first occurrence of *sub* or return -1 if not found
startswith(*sub*) endswith(*sub*)	Return True if *sub* is found at start or end respectively – otherwise return False
isalpha( ) isnumeric( ) isalnum( )	Return True if all characters are letters only, are numbers only, are letters or numbers only – otherwise return False
islower( ) isupper( ) istitle( )	Return True if string characters are lowercase, uppercase, or all first letters are uppercase only – otherwise return False
isspace( )	Return True if string contains only whitespace – otherwise return False
isdigit( ) isdecimal( )	Return True if string contains only digits or decimals – otherwise return False

Beware

A space character is not alphanumeric so **isalnum()** returns **False** when examining strings that contain spaces.

1 Start a new program by initializing a variable with a string of lowercase characters and spaces
string = 'coding for beginners in easy steps'

modify.py

2 Next, display the string capitalized, titled, and centered
print('\nCapitalized:\t' , **string.capitalize()**)
print('\nTitled:\t\t' , **string.title()**)
print('\nCentered:\t' , **string.center(30 , '*')**)

3 Now, display the string in all uppercase and merged with a sequence of two asterisks
print('\nUppercase:\t' , **string.upper()**)
print('\nJoined:\t\t' , **string.join('**')**)

4 Then, display the string padded with asterisks on the left
print('\nJustified:\t\t' ,**string.rjust(30 , '*')**)

5 Finally, display the string with all occurrences of the 's' character replaced by asterisks
print('\nReplaced:\t' , **string.replace('s' , '*')**)

6 Save then run the program – to see modified strings get displayed

```
Python Shell                                   –  □  ×
File  Edit  Shell  Debug  Options  Windows  Help
>>> ============= RESTART ================
>>>

Capitalized:       Coding for beginners in easy steps

Titled:            Coding For Beginners In Easy Steps

Centered:          coding for beginners in easy steps

Uppercase:         CODING FOR BEGINNERS IN EASY STEPS

Joined:            *coding for beginners in easy steps*

Justified:         coding for beginners in easy steps

Replaced:          coding for beginner* in ea*y *tep*
>>>|
```

With the **rjust()** function a RIGHT-justified string gets padding added to its LEFT, and with the **ljust()** function a LEFT-justified string gets padding added to its RIGHT.

117

Accessing files

The **__builtins__** module can be examined using the **dir()** function to reveal that it contains a **file** object that defines several methods for working with files, including **open()**, **read()**, **write()**, and **close()**.

Before a file can be read or written it firstly must always be opened using the **open()** function. This requires two string arguments to specify the name and location of the file, and one of the following "mode" specifiers in which to open the file:

File mode:	Operation:
r	Open an existing file to read
w	Open an existing file to write. Creates a new file if none exists or opens an existing file and discards all its previous contents
a	Append text. Opens or creates a text file for writing at the end of the file
r+	Open a text file to read from or write to
w+	Open a text file to write to or read from
a+	Open or creates a text file to read from or write to at the end of the file

Where the mode includes a **b** after any of the file modes listed above, the operation relates to a binary file rather than a text file. For example, **rb** or **w+b**

Once a file is opened and you have a **file** object and can get various information related to that file from its properties:

Property:	Description:
name	Name of the opened file
mode	Mode in which the file was opened
closed	Status Boolean value of **True** or **False**
readable( )	Read permission Boolean value of **True** or **False**
writable( )	Write permission Boolean value of **True** or **False**

Beware

File mode parameters are string values so must be surrounded by quotes.

Hot tip

You can also use a **readlines()** function that returns a list of all lines.

118

1   Start a new program by creating a file object for a new text file named "example.txt" in which to write content
```python
file = open( 'example.txt' , 'w' )
```

access.py

2   Next, add statements to display the file name and mode
```python
print( 'File Name:' , file.name )
print( 'File Open Mode:' , file.mode )
```

3   Now, add statements to display the file access permissions
```python
print( 'Readable:' , file.readable() )
print( 'Writable:' , file.writable() )
```

4   Then, define a function to determine the file's status
```python
def get_status( f ) :
        if ( f.closed != False ) :
                return 'Closed'
        else :
                return 'Open'
```

5   Finally, add statements to display the current file status then close the file and display the file status once more
```python
print( 'File Status:' , get_status( file ) )
file.close()
print( '\nFile Status:' , get_status( file ) )
```

6   Save then run the program – to see a file get opened for writing, then see the file get closed

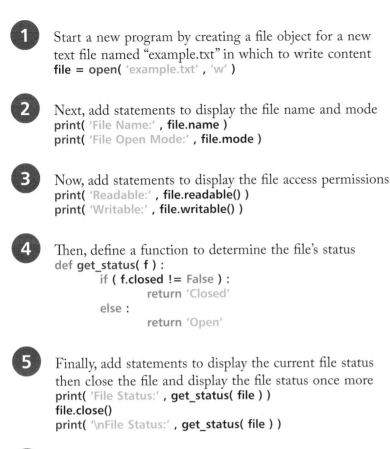

```
Python Shell                          – □ ×
File  Edit  Shell  Debug  Options  Windows  Help
>>> ============== RESTART ===============
>>>
File Name: example.txt
File Open Mode: w
Readable: False
Writable: True
File Status: Open

File Status: Closed
>>>
```

If your program tries to open a non-existent file in **r** mode the interpreter will report an error.

119

Manipulating content

Once a file has been successfully opened it can be read, or added to, or new text can be written in the file, depending on the mode specified in the call to the **open()** function. Following this, the open file must always be closed by calling the **close()** function.

As you might expect, the **read()** function returns the entire content of the file and the **write()** function adds content to the file.

You can quickly and efficiently read the entire contents in a loop, iterating line by line.

readwrite.py

 Start a new program by initializing a variable with a concatenated string containing newline characters
```
poem = 'I never saw a man who looked\n'
poem += 'With such a wistful eye\n'
poem += 'Upon that little tent of blue\n'
poem += 'Which prisoners call the sky\n'
```

 Next, add a statement to create a file object for a new text file named "poem.txt" to write content into
```
file = open( 'poem.txt' , 'w' )
```

 Now, add statements to write the string contained in the variable into the text file, then close that file
```
file.write( poem )
file.close()
```

 Then, add a statement to create a file object for the existing text file "poem.txt" to read from
```
file = open( 'poem.txt' , 'r' )
```

 Now, add statements to display the contents of the text file, then close that file
```
for line in file :
        print( line , end = '' )
file.close()
```

Save then run the program – to see the file created and read out to display

Beware

Writing to an existing file will automatically overwrite its contents!

```
Python Shell                          - □ ×
File  Edit  Shell  Debug  Options  Windows  Help
>>> ============= RESTART =============
>>>
I never saw a man who looked
With such a wistful eye
Upon that little tent of blue
Which prisoners call the sky
>>>
```

7 Launch the Notepad text editor to confirm the new text file exists and reveal its contents written by the program

```
poem.txt - Notepad                    - □ ×
File  Edit  Format  View  Help
I never saw a man who looked
With such a wistful eye
Upon that little tent of blue
Which prisoners call the sky
```

Suppress the default newline provided by the **print()** function where the strings themselves contain newlines.

8 Now, add statements at the end of the program to append a citation to the text file then save the script file again
```
file = open( 'poem.txt' , 'a' )
file.write( '(Oscar Wilde)' )
file.close()
```

9 Save then run the program again to re-write the text file then view its contents in Notepad – to see the citation now appended after the original text content

You can also use the file object's **readlines()** function that returns a list of all lines in a file – one line per element.

```
poem.txt - Notepad                    - □ ×
File  Edit  Format  View  Help
I never saw a man who looked
With such a wistful eye
Upon that little tent of blue
Which prisoners call the sky
(Oscar Wilde)
```

Updating content

A file object's **read()** function will, by default, read the entire contents of the file from the very beginning, at index position zero, to the very end – at the index position of the final character. Optionally, the **read()** function can accept an integer argument to specify how many characters it should read.

The position within the file, from which to read or at which to write, can be finely controlled by the file object's **seek()** function. This accepts an integer argument specifying how many characters to move position as an offset from the start of the file.

The current position within a file can be discovered at any time by calling the file object's **tell()** function to return an integer location.

When working with file objects it is good practice to use the Python **with** keyword to group the file operational statements within a block. This technique ensures that the file is properly closed after operations end, even if an exception is raised on the way, and much shorter than writing equivalent **try except** blocks.

update.py

 Start a new program by assigning a string value to a variable containing text to be written in a file
text = 'The political slogan "Workers Of The World Unite!" \nis from The Communist Manifesto.'

 Next, add statements to write the text string into a file and display the file's current status in the "with" block
with open('update.txt' , 'w' **) as file :**
      file.write(text)
      print('\nFile Now Closed?:' **, file.closed)**

 Now, add a non-indented statement after the "with" code block to display the file's new status
print('File Now Closed?:' **, file.closed)**

 Then, re-open the file and display its contents to confirm it now contains the entire text string
with open('update.txt' , 'r+' **) as file :**
      text = file.read()
      print('\nString:' **, text)**

5 Next, add indented statements to display the current file position, then reposition and display that new position

```
print( '\nPosition In File Now:' , file.tell() )
position = file.seek( 33 )
print( 'Position In File Now:' , file.tell() )
```

6 Now, add an indented statement to overwrite the text from the current file position

```
file.write( 'All Lands' )
```

7 Then, add indented statements to reposition in the file once more and overwrite the text from the new position

```
file.seek( 61 )
file.write( 'the tombstone of Karl Marx.' )
```

8 Finally, add indented statements to return to the start of the file and display its entire updated contents

```
file.seek( 0 )
text = file.read()
print( '\nString:' , text )
```

9 Save then run the program – to see the file strings get updated

Hot tip

The **seek()** function may optionally accept a second argument value of **0**, **1**, or **2** to move the specified number of characters from the start, current, or end position respectively – zero is the default start position.

123

```
                     Python Shell              –  □  ×
File  Edit  Shell  Debug  Options  Windows  Help
>>> ============= RESTART =============
>>>

File Now Closed?: False
File Now Closed?: True

String: The political slogan "Workers Of The World Unite!"
is from The Communist Manifesto.

Position In File Now: 85
Position In File Now: 33

String: The political slogan "Workers Of All Lands Unite!"
is from the tombstone of Karl Marx.
>>>
```

Don't forget

As with strings, the first character in a file is at index position zero – not at index position one.

Summary

- Strings can be manipulated by operators for concatenation + , to join strings together, and for repetition * of strings

- Strings can be manipulated by operators for slice [ ], and range slice [:] , that reference the index number of string characters

- Strings can be manipulated by membership operators **in** and **not in** that seek to match a specified character within a string

- The **r** (or **R**) raw string operator can be placed immediately before a string to suppress any escape characters it contains

- A "docstring" is a descriptive string within triple quote marks at the start of a module, class, or function, to define its purpose

- The **_doc_** attribute can be used to reference the string description within a docstring

- The **_builtins_** module can be examined using the **dir()** function to reveal the names of default functions and variables

- A **str** object has a **format()** function for string formatting and many functions for string modification, such as **capitalize()**

- Replacement fields in a string to be formatted using the format function are denoted in a comma-separated list by **{ }** braces

- Strings can also be formatted using the C-style **%s** substitution operator to mark places in a string where text is to be inserted

- A file object has **open()**, **read()**, **write()**, and **close()** functions for working with files, and features that describe the file properties

- The **open()** function must specify a file name string argument and a file mode string parameter, such as **'r'** to read the file

- A opened file object has information properties that reveal its current status, such as **mode** and **readable()** values

- Position in a file, at which to read or write, can be specified with the **seek()** method and reported by the **tell()** function

- The Python **with** keyword groups file operational statements within a block and automatically closes an open file

10 Programming objects

This chapter demonstrates how to code virtual objects into your programs.

Defining classes

The real-world objects that surround us each have attributes and behaviors we can describe. For example, a car might be described with a color attribute "red" and an "acceleration" behavior. Programming objects are like virtual representations of real-world objects that describe attributes and behaviors in a "class" structure.

A "class" is a specified prototype describing a set of properties that characterize an object. Each class has a data structure that can contain both functions and variables to characterize the object. The properties of a class are referred to as its data "members". Class function members are known as its "methods", and class variable members (declared within a class structure but outside any method definitions) are known as its "attributes". Class members can be referenced throughout a program using dot notation, suffixing the member name after the class name, with syntax of *class-name.method-name()* or *class-name.attribute-name*.

A class declaration begins with the **class** keyword, followed by a programmer-specified name (adhering to the usual Python naming conventions but beginning in uppercase) then a : colon. Next come indented statements, optionally specifying a class document string, class variable attribute declarations, and class method definitions – so the class block syntax looks like this:

class ClassName :

    ''' class-documentation-string '''

    class-variable-declarations

    class-method-definitions

The class declaration, which specifies its attributes and methods, is a blueprint from which working copies ("instances") can be made. All variables declared within method definitions are known as "instance" variables and are only available locally within the method in which they are declared – they cannot be directly referenced outside the class structure.

Typically, instance variables contain data passed by the caller when an instance copy of the class is created. As this data is only available locally for internal use it is effectively hidden from the rest of the program. This technique of data "encapsulation" ensures that data is securely stored within the class structure and is the first principle of Object Oriented Programming (OOP).

Hot tip

It is conventional to begin class names with an uppercase character and object names with lowercase.

126

All properties of a class are referenced internally by the dot notation prefix **self** – so an attribute named "sound" is **self.sound**. Additionally, all method definitions in a class must have **self** as their first parameter – so a method named "talk" is **talk(self)**.

When a class instance is created, a special **_init_(self)** method is automatically called. Subsequent parameters can be added in its parentheses if values are to be passed to initialize its attributes.

A complete Python class declaration could look like this example:

```
class Critter :

        ''' A base class for all critter properties. '''

        count = 0

        def _init_( self , chat ) :

                self.sound = chat
                Critter.count += 1

        def talk( self ) :

                return self.sound
```

It is useful to examine the class components of this example:

Don't forget

The class documentation string can be accessed via the special **_doc_** docstring attribute with *Classname._doc_* .

- The variable **count** is a class variable whose integer value gets shared among all instances of this class – this value can be referenced as **Critter.count** from inside or outside the class

- The first method **_init_()** is the initialization method that is automatically called when an instance of the class is created

- The **_init_()** method in this case initializes an instance variable **sound,** with a value passed from the **chat** parameter, and increments the value of the **count** class variable whenever an instance of this class is created

- The second method **talk()** is declared like a regular function except the first parameter is **self** which is automatically incorporated – no value needs to be passed from the caller

- The **talk()** method in this case simply returns the value encapsulated in the **sound** instance variable

Hot tip

While a program class cannot perfectly emulate a real-world object, the aim is to encapsulate all relevant attributes and actions.

Copying instances

An "instance" of a class object is simply a copy of the prototype created by calling that class name's constructor and specifying the required number of parameters within its parentheses. The call's arguments must match those specified by the **__init__()** method definition – other than a value for the internal **self** parameter.

The class instance object returned by the constructor is assigned to a variable using the syntax *instance-name = ClassName(args)*.

Dot notation can be used to reference the methods and class variable attributes of an instance object by suffixing their name as *instance-name.method-name()* or *instance-name.attribute-name*.

Typically, a base class can be defined as a Python module file so it can be imported into other scripts where instance objects can be easily created from the "master" class prototype.

A constructor creates a class instance using the class name followed by parentheses containing any required parameters.

Bird.py

① Start a new class file by declaring a new class with a descriptive document string
```
class Bird :
```

   ```
   '''A base class to define bird properties.'''
   ```

② Next, add an indented statement to declare and initialize a class variable attribute with an integer zero value
```
count = 0
```

③ Now, define the intializer class method to initialize an instance variable and to increment the class variable
```
def __init__( self , chat ) :
```

   ```
   self.sound = chat
   Bird.count += 1
   ```

④ Finally, add a class method to return the value of the instance variable when called – then save this class file
```
def talk( self ) :
```

   ```
   return self.sound
   ```

You must not pass an argument value for the self parameter as this is automatically incorporated by Python.

...cont'd

5 Start a program by making features of the class file available then display its document string
```
from Bird import *
print( '\nClass Instances Of:\n' , Bird.__doc__ )
```

instance.py

6 Next, add a statement to create an instance of the class and pass a string argument value to its instance variable
```
polly = Bird( 'Squawk, squawk!' )
```

7 Now, display this instance variable value and call the class method to display the common class variable value
```
print( '\nNumber Of Birds:' , polly.count )
print( 'Polly Says:' , polly.talk() )
```

Bird instance – polly

8 Create a second instance of the class passing a different string argument value to its instance variable
```
harry = Bird( 'Tweet, tweet!' )
```

9 Finally, display this instance variable value and call the class method to display the common class variable value
```
print( '\nNumber Of Birds:' , harry.count )
print( 'Harry Says:' , harry.talk() )
```

Bird instance – harry

10 Save both files then run the program – to see two instances of the Bird class get created

```
┌─────────────────────────────────────────────┐
│ 📝            Python Shell          – □ ✕     │
├─────────────────────────────────────────────┤
│ File  Edit  Shell  Debug  Options  Windows  Help │
│ >>> ============= RESTART ============= ▲    │
│ >>>                                           │
│                                               │
│ Class Instances Of:                           │
│  A base class to define bird properties.      │
│                                               │
│ Number Of Birds: 1                            │
│ Polly Says: Squawk, squawk!                   │
│                                               │
│ Number Of Birds: 2                            │
│ Harry Says: Tweet, tweet!                     │
│ >>> |                                         │
└─────────────────────────────────────────────┘
```

Beware

The class variable **count** can also be referenced with **Bird.count** but the encapsulated instance variable **sound** can only be accessed by calling an instance's **talk()** method.

Addressing properties

An attribute of a class instance can be added, modified, or removed at any time using dot notation to address the attribute. Making a statement that assigns a value to an attribute will update the value contained within an existing attribute or create a new attribute of the specified name containing the assigned value:

instance-name.attribute-name = value
del *instance-name.attribute-name*

Alternatively, you can use the following Python built-in functions to add, modify, or remove an instance variable:

The attribute name specified to these built-in functions must be enclosed within quotes.

- **getattr(** *instance-name* , *'attribute-name'* **)** – return the attribute value of the class instance

- **hasattr(** *instance-name* , *'attribute-name'* **)** – return **True** if the attribute value exists in the instance, otherwise return **False**

- **setattr(** *instance-name* , *'attribute-name'* , *value* **)** – update the existing attribute value or create a new attribute in the instance

- **delattr(** *instance-name* , *'attribute-name'* **)** – remove the attribute from the instance

The name of attributes automatically supplied by Python always begin with an underscore character to notionally indicate "privacy" – so these should not be modified, or removed. You can add your own attributes named in this way to indicate privacy if you wish, but in reality these can be modified like any other attribute.

130

1 Start a new program by making features of the Bird class available that was created on page 128
from Bird import *

address.py

2 Next, create an instance of the class then add a new attribute with an assigned value using dot notation
chick = Bird('Cheep, cheep!' **)**
chick.age = '1 week'

3 Now, display the values in both instance variable attributes
print('\nChick Says:' , chick.talk() **)**
print('Chick Age:' , chick.age **)**

4 Then, modify the new attribute using dot notation and display its new value
```
chick.age = '2 weeks'
print( 'Chick Now:' , chick.age )
```

5 Next, modify the new attribute once more, this time using a built-in function
```
setattr( chick , 'age' , '3 weeks' )
```

Bird instance – chick

6 Now, display a list of all non-private instance attributes and their respective values using a built-in function
```
print( '\nChick Attributes...' )
for attrib in dir( chick ) :
        if attrib[0] != '_' :
                print( attrib , ':' , getattr( chick , attrib ) )
```

7 Finally, remove the new attribute and confirm its removal using a built-in function
```
delattr( chick , 'age' )
print( '\nChick age Attribute?' , hasattr( chick , 'age' ) )
```

8 Save then run the program – to see the instance attributes get addressed

```
        Python Shell                                  –  □  ×
File  Edit  Shell  Debug  Options  Windows  Help
>>> ============== RESTART ===============
>>>

Chick Says: Cheep, cheep!
Chick Age: 1 week
Chick Now: 2 weeks

Chick Attributes...
age : 3 weeks
count : 1
sound : Cheep, cheep!
talk : <bound method Bird.talk of
      <Bird.Bird object at 0x0357E990>>

Chick age Attribute? False
>>>
```

Don't forget

This loop skips any attribute whose name begins with an underscore, so "private" attributes will not get displayed in the list.

Deriving classes

A Python class can be created as a brand new class, like those in previous examples, or can be "derived" from an existing class. Importantly, a derived class inherits members of the parent (base) class from which it is derived – in addition to its own members.

The ability to inherit members from a base class allows derived classes to be created that share certain common properties, which have been defined in the base class. For example, a "Polygon" base class may define width and height properties that are common to all polygons. Classes of "Rectangle" and Triangle" could be derived from the Polygon class – inheriting width and height properties, in addition to their own members defining their unique features.

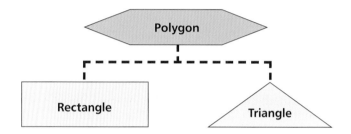

The virtue of inheritance is extremely powerful and is the second principle of Object Oriented Programming (OOP).

A derived class declaration adds ( ) parentheses after its class name specifying the name of its parent base class.

Polygon.py

1 Create a new class file that declares a base class with two class variables and a method to set their values

```python
class Polygon :
    width = 0
    height = 0
    def set_values( self , width , height ) :
        Polygon.width = width
        Polygon.height = height
```

Rectangle.py

2 Next, create a class file that declares a derived class with a method to return manipulated class variable values

```python
from Polygon import *

class Rectangle( Polygon ) :
    def area( self ) :
        return self.width * self.height
```

3 Now, create another class file that declares a derived class with a method to return manipulated class variable values

```
from Polygon import *

class Triangle( Polygon ) :
        def area( self ) :
                return ( self.width * self.height ) / 2
```

Triangle.py

4 Save the three class files then start a new program by making features of both derived classes available

```
from Rectangle import *
from Triangle import *
```

inherit.py

5 Next, create an instance of each derived class

```
rect = Rectangle()
trey = Triangle()
```

6 Now, call the class method inherited from the base class, passing arguments to assign to the class variables

```
rect.set_values( 4 , 5 )
trey.set_values( 4 , 5 )
```

Hot tip

A class declaration can derive from more than one class by listing multiple base classes in the parentheses after its name in the declaration.

7 Finally, display the result of manipulating the class variables inherited from the base class

```
print( 'Rectangle Area:' , rect.area() )
print( 'Triangle Area:' , trey.area() )
```

8 Save then run the program – to see output get displayed using inherited features

```
Python Shell                              – □ ×
File  Edit  Shell  Debug  Options  Windows  Help
>>> ============= RESTART =============
>>>
Rectangle Area: 20
Triangle Area: 10.0
>>>
```

Beware

Don't confuse class instances and derived classes – an instance is a copy of a class, whereas a derived class is a new class that inherits properties of the base class from which it is derived.

Overriding methods

A method can be declared in a derived class to override a matching method in the base class – if both method declarations have the same name and the same number of listed parameters. This effectively hides the base class method as it becomes inaccessible unless it is called explicitly, using the base class name for identification.

Where a method in a base class supplies a default parameter value this can be used in an explicit call to the base method or alternative values can be supplied by overriding methods.

Person.py

1 Create a new class file that declares a base class with an initializer method to set an instance variable and a second method to display that variable value

```python
class Person :

    '''A base class to define Person properties.'''

    def __init__( self , name ) :
        self.name = name

    def speak( self , msg  = '(Calling The Base Class)' ) :
        print( self.name , msg )
```

Man.py

2 Next, create a class file that declares a derived class with a method that overrides the second base class method

```python
from Person import *

    '''A derived class to define Man properties.'''

class Man( Person ) :
    def speak( self , msg ) :
        print( self.name , ':\n\tHello!' , msg )
```

Hombre.py

3 Now, create another class file that also declares a derived class with a method that once again overrides the same method in the base class

```python
from Person import *

    '''A derived class to define Hombre properties.'''

class Hombre( Person ) :
    def speak( self , msg ) :
        print( self.name , ':\n\tHola!' , msg )
```

4 Save the three class files then start a new program by making features of both derived classes available
```
from Man import *
from Hombre import *
```

override.py

5 Next, create an instance of each derived class, initializing the "name" instance variable attribute
```
guy_1 = Man( 'Richard' )
guy_2 = Hombre( 'Ricardo' )
```

6 Now, call the overriding methods of each derived class, assigning different values to the "msg" parameter
```
guy_1.speak( 'It\'s a beautiful evening.\n' )
guy_2.speak( 'Es una tarde hermosa.\n' )
```

Man – Richard
Hombre – Ricardo

7 Finally, explicitly call the base class method, passing a reference to each derived class – but none for the "msg" variable so its default value will be used
```
Person.speak( guy_1 )
Person.speak( guy_2 )
```

8 Save then run the program – to see output from overriding and base class methods

```
 ┌──────────────────────────────────────────────────┐
 │ [≣]            Python Shell         — □  [x]       │
 ├──────────────────────────────────────────────────┤
 │ File  Edit  Shell  Debug  Options  Windows  Help  │
 │ >>> ============ RESTART =============== ▲         │
 │ >>>                                                │
 │ Richard :                                          │
 │         Hello! It's a beautiful evening.           │
 │                                                    │
 │ Ricardo :                                          │
 │         Hola! Es una tarde hermosa.                │
 │                                                    │
 │ Richard (Calling The Base Class)                   │
 │ Ricardo (Calling The Base Class)                   │
 │ >>> |                                              │
 └──────────────────────────────────────────────────┘
```

Don't forget

The method declaration in the derived class must exactly match that in the base class to override it.

Applying sense

The three cornerstones of Object Oriented Programming (OOP) are encapsulation, inheritance, and polymorphism. Examples earlier in this chapter have demonstrated how data can be encapsulated within a Python class, and how derived classes inherit the properties of their base class. This example introduces the final cornerstone principle of polymorphism.

The term "polymorphism" (from Greek, meaning "many forms") describes the ability to assign a different meaning, or purpose, to an entity according to its context.

In Python, the + character entity can be described as polymorphic because it represents either the arithmetical addition operator, in the context of numerical operands, or the string concatenation operator in the context of character operands.

Perhaps more importantly, Python class methods can also be polymorphic because the Python language uses "duck typing" – meaning... if it walks like a duck, swims like a duck, and quacks like a duck, then that bird is reckoned to be a duck.

In a duck-typed language you can create a function to take an object of any type and call that object's methods. If the object does indeed have the called methods (is reckoned to be a duck) they are executed, otherwise the function signals a run-time error.

Like-named methods of multiple classes can be created and instances of those classes will execute the associated version.

Duck.py

1   Create a new class file that declares a class with methods to display strings unique to the class

```
class Duck :
        def talk( self ) :
                print( '\nDuck Says: Quack!' )
        def coat( self ) :
                print( 'Duck Wears: Feathers' )
```

Mouse.py

2   Next, create a class file that declares a class with like-named methods but to display strings unique to this class

```
class Mouse :
        def talk( self ) :
                print( '\nMouse Says: Squeak!' )
        def coat( self ) :
                print( 'Mouse Wears: Fur' )
```

3   Save the two class files then start a new program by making features of both classes available
```
from Duck import *
from Mouse import *
```

polymorph.py

4   Next, define a function that accepts any single object as its parameter and attempts to call methods of that object
```
def describe( object ) :
        object.talk()
        object.coat()
```

Duck – donald

5   Now, create an instance object of each class
```
donald = Duck()
mickey = Mouse()
```

6   Finally, add statements to call the function and pass each instance object to it as an argument
```
describe( donald )
describe( mickey )
```

7   Save then run the program – to see the methods of the associated versions get called

Mouse – mickey

```
                    Python Shell            –  □  ×
File  Edit  Shell  Debug  Options  Windows  Help
>>> ============== RESTART ===============
>>>

Duck Says: Quack!
Duck Wears: Feathers

Mouse Says: Squeak!
Mouse Wears: Fur
>>>|
```

Don't forget

A class can have only one method with a given name – method overloading is not supported in Python.

Object Oriented Programming with Python allows data encapsulation, inheritance, and polymorphism. Base class methods can be overridden by like-named methods in derived classes. Python does not, however, support the technique of "overloading" found in other languages – in which methods of the same name can be created with different parameter lists in a single class.

Summary

- Programming objects are like virtual representations of real-world objects describing attributes and behaviors in a "class"

- A class is a data structure prototype describing object properties with its methods and attribute members

- Each class declaration begins with the **class** keyword and is followed by an indented code block that may contain a class document string, class variables, and class methods

- Class variables have global scope but instance variables (declared within method definitions) have only local scope

- Instance variables encapsulate data securely in a class structure and are initialized when a class instance is created

- Properties of a class are referenced by dot notation and are addressed internally using the **self** prefix

- A class instance is a copy of the prototype that automatically calls its **__init__()** method when the instance is first created

- An attribute of a class can be added, modified, or removed using dot notation or manipulated using the built-in functions **getattr()**, **hasattr()**, **setattr()**, and **delattr()**

- The name of attributes automatically supplied by Python begin with an underscore character to notionally indicate privacy

- A derived class inherits the method and attribute members of the parent base class from which it is derived

- The declaration of a derived class must state the name of its parent base class in parentheses after its own class name

- A method of a derived class can override a matching method of the same name in its parent base class

- A method of a base class can be called explicitly using the base class name for identification

- Python is a duck-typed language that supports polymorphism for like-named methods of multiple classes

- The three cornerstones of Object Oriented Programming (OOP) are Encapsulation, Inheritance, and Polymorphism

11 Building interfaces

This chapter demonstrates how to code graphical windowed programs.

There can be only one call to the **Tk()** constructor and it must be at the start of the program code.

The **grid()** geometry manager method is demonstrated in the example on page 161.

Launching interfaces

The standard Python module that you can use to create graphical applications is called "tkinter" – a **tool**kit to **inter**face with the system GUI (Graphical User Interface).

The **tkinter** module can be imported into a program like any other module to provide attributes and methods for windowed apps. Every **tkinter** program must begin by calling the **Tk()** constructor to create a window object. The window's size can optionally be specified as a *'widthxheight'* string argument to the window object's **geometry()** method. Similarly, the window's title can be specified as a *'title'* string argument to the window object's **title()** method. If not specified, default size and title values will be used.

Every **tkinter** program must also call the window object's **mainloop()** method to capture events, such as when the user closes the window to quit the program. This loop should appear at the end of the program as it also handles window updates that may be implemented during execution.

With **tkinter**, all the graphical controls that can be included in the application window, such as buttons or checkboxes, are referred to as "widgets". Perhaps the simplest widget is a non-interactive label object that merely displays text or an image in the app interface. A label object can be created by specifying the window object's name and **text=***'string'* as arguments to a **Label()** constructor.

Once created, each widget, such as a label, must then be added to the window using one of these "geometry manager" methods:

- **pack()** – places the widget against a specified side of the window using **TOP**, **BOTTOM**, **LEFT**, or **RIGHT** constant values specified to its **side=** argument
- **place()** – places the widget at XY coordinates in the window using numerical values specified to its **x=** and **y=** arguments
- **grid()** – places the widget in a cell within the window using numerical values specified to **row=** and **column=** arguments

Optionally, the **pack()** method may include a **fill** argument to expand the widget in available space. For example, with **fill = 'x'**. Alternatively, the **pack()** method may include **padx** and **pady** arguments to expand the widget along an axis by a specified amount.

Start a new program with a statement to make the "tkinter" module GUI methods and attributes available
from tkinter import *

Next, add a statement to call upon a constructor to create a window object
window = Tk()

window.py

Now, add a statement to specify a title for this window
window.title('Label Example' **)**

Then, add a statement to call upon a constructor to create a label object
label = Label(window , text = 'Hello World!' **)**

Use the packer to add the label to the window with both horizontal and vertical padding for positioning
label.pack(padx = 200 , pady = 50)

Widgets will not appear in the window when running the program unless they have been added with a geometry manager.

Finally, add the mandatory statement to maintain the window by capturing events
window.mainloop()

Save then run the program – to see a window appear containing a label widget

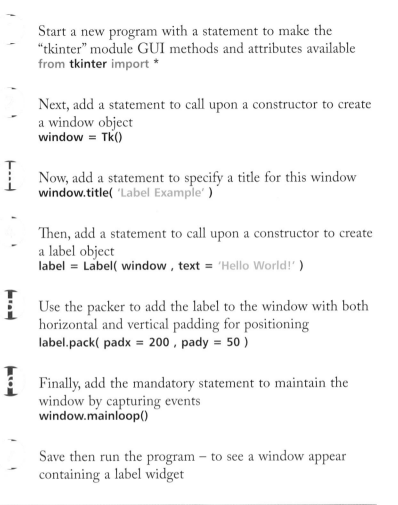

Responding buttons

A Button widget provides a graphical button in an application window that may contain either text or an image to convey the button's purpose. A button object is created by specifying the window name and options as arguments to a **Button()** constructor. Each option is specified as an option=value pair. The **command** option must always specify the name of a function or method to call when the user clicks that button. The most popular options are listed below, together with a brief description:

Option:	Description:
activebackground	Background color when the cursor is over
activeforeground	Foreground color when the cursor is over
bd	Border width in pixels (default is 2)
bg	Background color
command	Function to call when clicked
fg	Foreground color
font	Font for button label
height	Button height in text lines, or pixels for images
highlightcolor	Border color when in focus
image	Image to be displayed instead of text
justify	Multiple text lines as LEFT, CENTER, or RIGHT
padx	Horizontal padding
pady	Vertical padding
relief	Border style of SUNKEN, RIDGE, RAISED or GROOVE
state	Enabled status of NORMAL or DISABLED
underline	Index number in text of character to underline
width	Button width in letters, or pixels for images
wraplength	Length at which to wrap text

Hot tip

You can also call a button's **invoke()** method to, in turn, call the function nominated to its **command** option.

The values assigned to other options determine the widget's appearance. These can be altered by specifying a new option=value pair as an argument to the widget's **configure()** method. Additionally, a current option value can be retrieved by specifying its name as a string argument to the widget's **cget()** method.

...cont'd

button.py

1 Start a new program by making GUI features available, then create a window and specify a title
```
from tkinter import *
window = Tk()
window.title( 'Button Example' )
```

2 Next, create a button to exit the program when clicked
```
btn_end = Button( window , text = 'Close' , command=exit )
```

3 Now, add a function to toggle the window's background color when another button gets clicked
```
def tog() :
        if window.cget( 'bg' ) == 'yellow' :
                window.configure( bg = 'gray' )
        else :
                window.configure( bg = 'yellow' )
```

Beware

Only the function name is specified to the **command** option. Do not add trailing parentheses in the assignment.

4 Then, create a button to call the function when clicked
```
btn_tog = Button( window , text = 'Switch' , command=tog )
```

5 Add the buttons to the window with positional padding
```
btn_end.pack( padx = 150 , pady = 20 )
btn_tog.pack( padx = 150 , pady = 20 )
```

6 Finally, add the loop to capture this window's events
```
window.mainloop()
```

7 Save then run the program and click the button – to see the window's background color change

Hot tip

The 'gray' color is the original default color of the window.

143

Displaying messages

A program can display messages to the user by calling methods provided in the "tkinter.messagebox" module. This must be imported separately and its lengthy name can usefully be assigned a short alias by an **import as** statement.

A message box is created by supplying a box title and the message to be displayed as the two arguments to one of these methods:

Method:	Icon:	Buttons:
showinfo()		OK
showwarning()		OK
showerror()		OK
askquestion()		Yes (returns the string 'yes') and No (returns the string 'no')
askokcancel()		OK (returns 1) and Cancel
askyesno()		Yes (returns 1) and No
askretrycancel()		Retry (returns 1) and Cancel

Hot tip

Only the **askquestion()** method returns two values – the **askyesno()** No button and both Cancel buttons return nothing.

Those methods that produce a message box containing a single OK button return no value when the button gets clicked by the user. Those that do return a value can be used to perform conditional branching by testing that value.

...cont'd

1 Start a new program by making GUI features available and message box features available as a short alias
```
from tkinter import *
import tkinter.messagebox as box
```

message.py

2 Next, create a window object and specify a title
```
window = Tk()
window.title( 'Message Box Example' )
```

3 Add a function to display various message boxes
```
def dialog() :
        var = box.askyesno( 'Message Box' , 'Proceed?' )
        if var == 1 :
                box.showinfo( 'Yes Box', 'Proceeding...' )
        else :
                box.showwarning( 'No Box', 'Canceling...' )
```

4 Then, create a button to call the function when clicked
```
btn = Button( window , text = 'Click' , command=dialog )
```

5 Add the button to the window with positional padding
```
btn.pack( padx = 150 , pady = 50 )
```

Hot tip

Options can be added as a third argument to these method calls. For example, add **type='abortretryignore'** to get three buttons.

6 Finally, add the loop to capture this window's events
```
window.mainloop()
```

7 Save the file then run the program and click the button – to see the message boxes appear

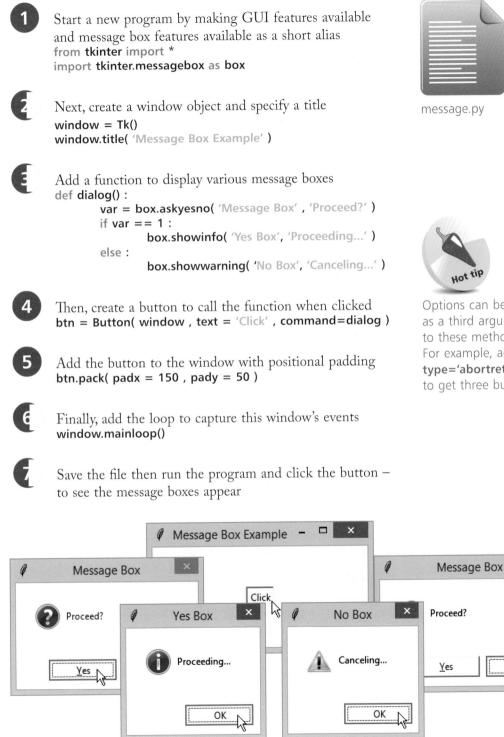

Gathering entries

An Entry widget provides a single-line input field in an application where the program can gather entries from the user. An entry object is created by specifying the name of its parent container, such as a window or frame name, and options as arguments to an **Entry()** constructor. Each option is specified as an option=value pair. Popular options are listed below, together with a brief description:

Option:	Description:
bd	Border width in pixels (default is 2)
bg	Background color
fg	Foreground color used to render the text
font	Font for the text
highlightcolor	Border color when in focus
selectbackground	Background color of selected text
selectforeground	Foreground color of selected text
show	Hide password characters with show='*'
state	Enabled status of NORMAL or DISABLED
width	Entry width in letters

Multiple widgets can be grouped in frames for better positioning. A frame object is created by specifying the name of the window to a **Frame()** constructor. The frame's name can then be specified as the first argument to the widget constructors to identify it as that widget's container.

When actually adding widgets to the frame, you can specify which side to pack them to in the frame with **TOP**, **BOTTOM**, **LEFT**, or **RIGHT** constants. For example, **entry.pack(side=LEFT)**.

Typically, an entry widget will appear alongside a label describing the type of input expected there from the user, or alongside a button widget that the user can click to perform some action on the data they have entered, so positioning in a frame is ideal.

Data currently entered into an entry widget can be retrieved by the program using that widget's **get()** method.

Hot tip

Use the Text widget instead of an Entry widget if you want to allow the user to enter multiple lines of text.

1 Start a new program by making GUI features available and message box features available as a short alias
```
from tkinter import *
import tkinter.messagebox as box
```

entry.py

2 Next, create a window object and specify a title
```
window = Tk()
window.title( 'Entry Example' )
```

3 Now, create a frame containing an entry field for input
```
frame = Frame( window )
entry = Entry( frame )
```

4 Then, add a function to display data currently entered
```
def dialog() :
        box.showinfo( 'Greetings' , 'Welcome ' + entry.get() )
```

5 Now, create a button to call the function when clicked
```
btn = Button( frame, text = 'Enter Name' , command=dialog )
```

6 Add the button and entry to the frame at set sides
```
btn.pack( side = RIGHT , padx = 5 )
entry.pack( side = LEFT )
frame.pack( padx = 20 , pady = 20 )
```

7 Finally, add the loop to capture this window's events
```
window.mainloop()
```

8 Save the file and run the program, then enter your name and click the button – to see a greeting message appear

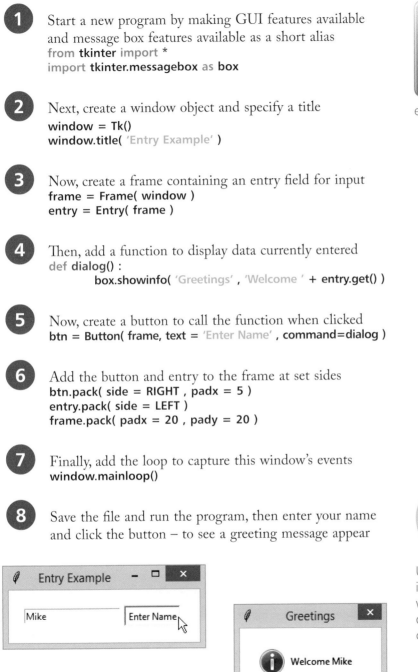

147

Hot tip

Use a Label widget instead of an Entry widget if you want to display text that the user cannot edit.

Listing options

A Listbox widget provides a list of items in an application from which the user can make a selection. A listbox object is created by specifying the name of its parent container, such as a window or frame name, and options as arguments to a **Listbox()** constructor. Popular options are listed below, together with a brief description:

Option:	Description:
bd	Border width in pixels (default is 2)
bg	Background color
fg	Foreground color used to render the text
font	Font for the text
height	Number of lines in list (default is 10)
selectbackground	Background color of selected text
selectmode	SINGLE (the default) or MULTIPLE selections
width	Listbox width in letters (default is 20)
yscrollcommand	Attach to a vertical scrollbar

With tkinter, a scrollbar is a separate widget that can be attached to Listbox, Text, Canvas and Entry widgets.

Items are added to the listbox by specifying a list index number and the item string as arguments to its **insert()** method.

You can retrieve any item from a listbox by specifying its index number within the parentheses of its **get()** method. Usefully, a listbox also has a **curselection()** method that returns the index number of the currently selected item, so this can be supplied as the argument to its **get()** method to retrieve the current selection.

listbox.py

1 Start a new program by making GUI features available and message box features available as a short alias
from **tkinter** import *
import **tkinter.messagebox** as **box**

2 Next, create a window object and specify a title
window = **Tk()**
window.**title(** 'Listbox Example' **)**

3 Now, create a frame to contain widgets
frame = **Frame(** window **)**

148

4 Create a listbox widget offering three list items
```
listbox = Listbox( frame )
listbox.insert( 1 , 'HTML5 in easy steps' )
listbox.insert( 2 , 'CSS3 in easy steps' )
listbox.insert( 3 , 'JavaScript in easy steps' )
```

5 Next, add a function to display a listbox selection
```
def dialog() :
        box.showinfo( 'Selection' , 'Your Choice: ' + \
        listbox.get( listbox.curselection() ) )
```

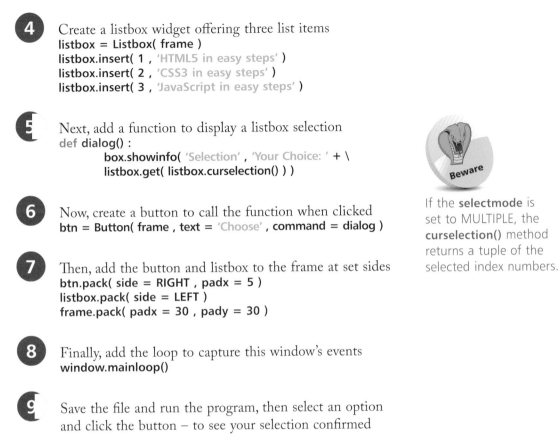

If the **selectmode** is set to MULTIPLE, the **curselection()** method returns a tuple of the selected index numbers.

6 Now, create a button to call the function when clicked
```
btn = Button( frame , text = 'Choose' , command = dialog )
```

7 Then, add the button and listbox to the frame at set sides
```
btn.pack( side = RIGHT , padx = 5 )
listbox.pack( side = LEFT )
frame.pack( padx = 30 , pady = 30 )
```

8 Finally, add the loop to capture this window's events
```
window.mainloop()
```

149

9 Save the file and run the program, then select an option and click the button – to see your selection confirmed

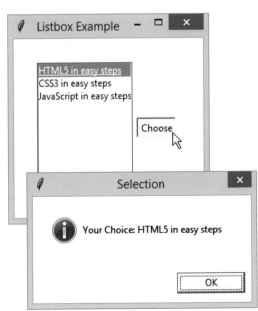

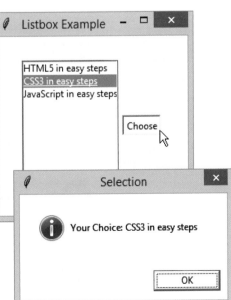

Polling radios

A Radiobutton widget provides a single item in an application that the user may select. Where a number of radio buttons are grouped together, the user may only select any one item in the group. With tkinter, radio button objects are grouped together when they nominate the same control variable object to assign a value to upon selection. An empty string variable object can be created for this purpose using the **StringVar()** constructor or an empty integer variable object using the **IntVar()** constructor.

A radio button object is created by specifying four arguments to a **Radiobutton()** constructor:

- Name of the parent container, such as the frame name
- Text for a display label, specified as a **text**=text pair
- Control variable object, specified as a **variable**=variable pair
- Value to be assigned, specified as a **value**=value pair

Each radio button object has a **select()** method that can be used to specify a default selection in a group of radio buttons when the program starts. A string value assigned by selecting a radio button can be retrieved from a string variable object by its **get()** method.

Beware

You cannot use a regular variable to store values assigned from a radio button selection – it must be an object.

radio.py

1 Start a new program by making GUI features available and message box features available as a short alias
```
from tkinter import *
import tkinter.messagebox as box
```

2 Next, create a window object and specify a title
```
window = Tk()
window.title( 'Radio Button Example' )
```

3 Now, create a frame to contain widgets
```
frame = Frame( window )
```

4 Then, construct a string variable object to store a selection
```
book = StringVar()
```

5 Next, create three radio button widgets whose value will be assigned to the string variable upon selection

```
radio_1 = Radiobutton( frame , text = 'HTML5' , \
        variable = book , value = 'HTML5 in easy steps' )
radio_2 = Radiobutton( frame , text = 'CSS3' , \
        variable = book , value = 'CSS3 in easy steps' )
radio_3 = Radiobutton( frame , text = 'JS' , \
        variable = book , value = 'JavaScript in easy steps' )
```

6 Now, add a statement to specify which radio button will be selected by default when the program starts

```
radio_1.select()
```

7 Then, add a function to display a radio button selection and a button to call this function

```
def dialog() :
        box.showinfo( 'Selection' , \
        'Your Choice: \n' + book.get() )
btn = Button( frame , text = 'Choose' , command = dialog )
```

8 Add the push button and radio buttons to the frame

```
btn.pack( side = RIGHT , padx = 5 )
radio_1.pack( side = LEFT )
radio_2.pack( side = LEFT )
radio_3.pack( side = LEFT )
frame.pack( padx = 30 , pady = 30 )
```

9 Finally, add the loop to capture this window's events

```
window.mainloop()
```

10 Save the file and run the program, then choose an option and click the button – to see your choice confirmed

Hot tip

A Radiobutton object has a **deselect()** method that can be used to cancel a selection programatically.

Checking boxes

A Checkbutton widget provides a single item in an application that the user may select. Where a number of check buttons appear together the user may select one or more items. Check button objects nominate an individual control variable object to assign a value to, whether checked or unchecked. An empty string variable object can be created for this using the **StringVar()** constructor or an empty integer variable object using the **IntVar()** constructor.

A check button object is created by specifying five arguments to a **Checkbutton()** constructor:

- Name of the parent container, such as the frame name
- Text for a display label, as a **text**=text pair
- Control variable object, as a **variable**=variable pair
- Value to assign if checked, as an **onvalue**=value pair
- Value to assign if unchecked, as an **offvalue**=value pair

An integer value assigned by a check button can be retrieved from a integer variable object by its **get()** method.

check.py

1 Start a new program by making GUI features available and message box features available as a short alias
```
from tkinter import *
import tkinter.messagebox as box
```

2 Next, create a window object and specify a title
```
window = Tk()
window.title( 'Check Button Example' )
```

3 Now, create a frame to contain widgets
```
frame = Frame( window )
```

4 Then, construct three integer variable objects to store values
```
var_1 = IntVar()
var_2 = IntVar()
var_3 = IntVar()
```

5 Create three check button widgets whose values will be assigned to the integer variable, whether checked or not
```
book_1 = Checkbutton( frame , text = 'HTML5' , \
        variable = var_1 , onvalue = 1 , offvalue = 0 )
book_2 = Checkbutton( frame , text = 'CSS3' , \
        variable = var_2 , onvalue = 1 , offvalue = 0 )
book_3 = Checkbutton( frame , text = 'JS' , \
        variable = var_3 , onvalue = 1 , offvalue = 0 )
```

6 Next, add a function to display a check button selection
```
def dialog() :
        s = 'Your Choice:'
        if var_1.get() == 1 : s += '\nHTML5 in easy steps'
        if var_2.get() == 1 : s += '\nCSS3 in easy steps'
        if var_3.get() == 1 : s += '\nJavaScript in easy steps'
        box.showinfo( 'Selection' , s )
```

7 Now, create a button to call the function when clicked
```
btn = Button( frame , text = 'Choose' , command = dialog )
```

8 Then, add the push button and check buttons to the frame
```
btn.pack( side = RIGHT , padx = 5 )
book_1.pack( side = LEFT )
book_2.pack( side = LEFT )
book_3.pack( side = LEFT )
frame.pack( padx = 30, pady = 30 )
```

9 Finally, add the loop to capture this window's events
```
window.mainloop()
```

10 Save the file and run the program, then check boxes and click the button – to see your selection confirmed

A Checkbutton object has **select()** and **deselect()** methods that can be used to turn the state on or off. For example, **check_1. select()**.

The state of any Checkbutton object can be reversed by calling its **toggle()** method.

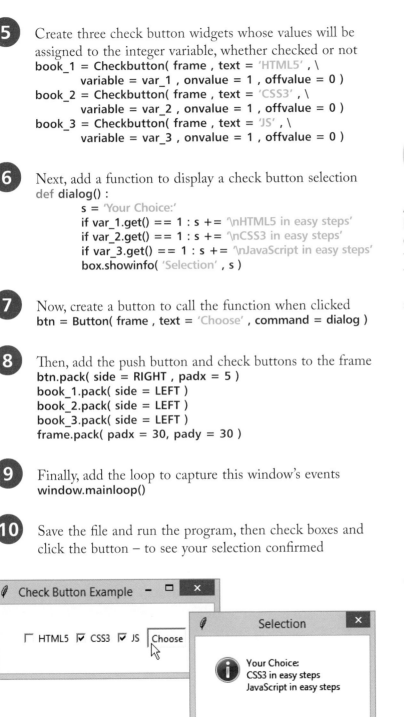

Adding images

With the **tkinter** module, images in GIF or PGM/PPM file formats can be displayed on Label, Button, Text and Canvas widgets using the **PhotoImage()** constructor to create image objects. This simply requires a single **file=** argument to specify the image file. Interestingly, it also has a **subsample()** method that can scale down a specified image by stating a sample value to **x=** and **y=** arguments. For example, values of **x=2, y=2** samples every second pixel – so the image object is half-size of the original.

Once an image object has been created it can be added to a Label or Button constructor statement by an **image=** option.

Text objects have an **image_create()** method with which to embed an image into the text field. This requires two arguments to specify location and **image=**. For example, **'1.0'** specifies the first line and first character.

Canvas objects have a **create_image()** method that requires two arguments to specify location and **image=**. Here the location sets the x,y coordinates on the canvas at which to paint the image.

Hot tip

The PhotoImage class also has a **zoom()** method that will double the image size with the same **x=2,y=2** values.

image.py

python.gif
(200 x 200)

 Start a new program by making GUI methods and attributes available, then create a window object and specify a title
```
from tkinter import *
window = Tk()
window.title( 'Image Example' )
```

 Now, create an image object from a local image file
```
img = PhotoImage( file = 'python.gif' )
```

 Then, create a label object to display the image above a colored background
```
label = Label( window , image = img , bg = 'yellow' )
```

 Create a half-size image object from the first image object
```
small_img = PhotoImage.subsample( img , x = 2 , y = 2 )
```

 Now, create a button to display the small image
```
btn = Button( window , image = small_img )
```

6 Create a text field and embed the small image, then insert some text after it
```
txt = Text( window , width = 25 , height = 7 )
txt.image_create( '1.0' , image = small_img )
txt.insert( '1.1', 'Python Fun!' )
```

7 Create a canvas and paint the small image above a colored background, then paint a diagonal line over the top of it
```
can = \
Canvas( window , width = 100 , height = 100 , bg = 'cyan' )
can.create_image( ( 50 , 50 ), image = small_img )
can.create_line( 0 , 0 , 100 , 100, width = 25 , fill = 'yellow' )
```

8 Then, add the widgets to the window
```
label.pack( side = TOP )
btn.pack( side = LEFT , padx = 10 )
txt.pack( side = LEFT )
can.pack( side = LEFT, padx = 10 )
```

9 Finally, add the loop to capture this window's events
```
window.mainloop()
```

10 Save the file then run the program – to see the image on the Label, Button, Text and Canvas widgets

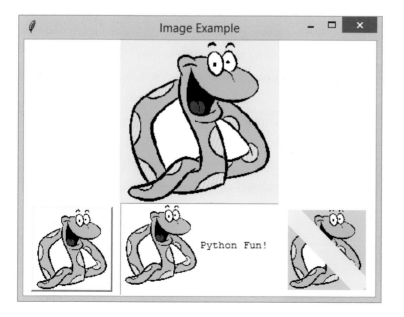

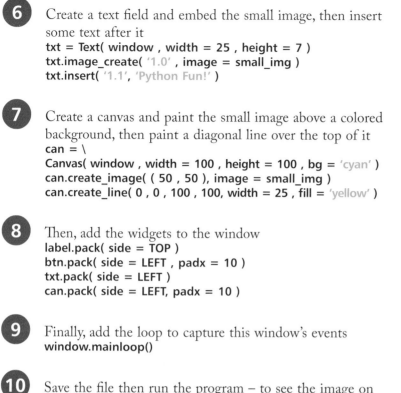

Notice that the Text method is **image_create()** but the Canvas method is **create_image()** – similar yet different.

Text and Canvas widgets are both powerful and flexible – discover more online at **https://docs.python.org/3/library/tkinter.html**

Summary

- The **tkinter** module can be imported into a Python program to provide attributes and methods for windowed applications
- Every **tkinter** program must begin by calling **Tk()** to create a window and call its **mainloop()** method to capture events
- The window object's title is specified by its **title()** method
- A label widget is created by specifying the name of its parent container and its text as arguments to the **Label()** constructor
- Widgets can be added to an application using the **pack()**, **grid()** or **place()** geometry managers
- A button widget is created by specifying the name of its parent container, its text, and the name of a function to call when the user pushes it, as arguments to the **Button()** constructor
- The **tkinter.messagebox** module can be imported into a Python program to provide attributes and methods for message boxes
- Message boxes that ask the user to make a choice return a value to the program for conditional branching
- The **Frame()** constructor creates a container in which multiple widgets can be grouped for better positioning
- The **Entry()** constructor creates a single line text field whose current contents can be retrieved by its **get()** method
- Items are added to a **Listbox** object by its **insert()** method and retrieved by specifying their index number to its **get()** method
- **Radiobutton** and **Checkbutton** objects store values in the **StringVar** or **IntVar** object nominated by their **variable** attribute
- The **PhotoImage()** constructor creates an image object that has a **subsample**() method which can scale down the image
- Images can be added to **Button** and **Label** objects, embedded in **Text** objects, and painted on **Canvas** objects

12 Developing apps

This chapter brings together elements from previous chapters to develop a windowed application.

Generating randoms

The graphical application developed on subsequent pages of this book will generate six random numbers within a specific range. Initially, its functionality can be developed as a console application then transferred later to illustrate how it can be applied to graphical widget components.

The standard Python library has a **random** module that provides methods to generate pseudo-random numbers. The current system time is used by default to "seed" the random generator whenever it gets initialized – so it does not repeat its selections.

Beware

Floating-point numbers cast from the **float** data type to the **int** data type by the built-in **int()** function get truncated at the decimal point.

A pseudo-random floating-point number from 0.0 to 1.0 can be generated by calling the **random()** method from the **random** module. The range of generated numbers can be modified using the * multiplication operator to specify a maximum value and can be rounded down to integer values using the built-in **int()** function. For example, to generate an integer within the range of zero to nine:

int(random.random() * 10)

Or to generate a whole number within the range of 1 to 10:

int(random.random() * 10) + 1

This statement could be used in a loop to generate multiple random integers within a given range but any number may be repeated in that output – there is no guaranteed uniqueness. Instead, multiple unique random integers within a given range can be generated by the **sample()** method from the **random** module. This requires two arguments to specify the range and the number of unique integers to be returned. It is convenient to use the built-in **range()** function to specify a maximum value. For example, to generate six unique numbers within the range of 1 to 9:

Don't forget

The **range()** function can specify start and end values. If no starting value is supplied, zero is assumed by default.

random.sample(range(10) , 6)

Or to generate six unique numbers within the range of 1 to 10:

random.sample(range(1 , 11) , 6)

This technique could represent a random lottery entry by choosing, say, six unique numbers between 1 and 49.

...cont'd

1 Start a new program by importing two functions from the "random" module
```
from random import random , sample
```

sample.py

2 Next, assign a random floating-point number to a variable then display its value
```
num = random()
print( 'Random Float 0.0-1.0 : ' , num )
```

3 Now, multiply the floating-point number and cast it to become an integer, then display its value
```
num = int( num * 10 )
print( 'Random Integer  0 - 9 : ' , num )
```

4 Add a loop to assign multiple random integers to a list, then display the list items
```
nums = [] ; i = 0
while i < 6 :
        nums.append( int( random() * 10 ) + 1 )
        i += 1
print( 'Random Multiple Integers 1-10 :' , nums )
```

5 Finally, assign multiple unique random integers to the list, then display the list items
```
nums = sample( range( 1, 49 ) , 6 )
print( 'Random Integer Sample 1 - 49 : ' , nums )
```

6 Save the file, then run the program several times – to see the generated random numbers

```
                        Python Shell              –  □  ✕
 File  Edit  Shell  Debug  Options  Windows  Help
>>>
Random Float 0.0-1.0 :  0.6030055202135008
Random Integer 0 - 9 :  6
Random Multiple Integers 1-10:  [4, 7, 5, 1, 1, 8]
Random Integer Sample 1 - 49 :  [21, 18, 5, 45, 29, 30]
>>> ================ RESTART ===========
>>>
Random Float 0.0-1.0 :  0.308325899426137
Random Integer 0 - 9 :  3
Random Multiple Integers 1-10:  [2, 4, 7, 6, 5, 10]
Random Integer Sample 1 - 49 :  [3, 1, 28, 31, 23, 35]
```

Hot tip

The **random.sample()** function returns a list but does not actually replace any elements in the specified range.

Planning needs

When creating a new graphical application it is useful to first spend some time planning its design. Clearly define the program's precise purpose, decide what application functionality will be required, then decide what interface widgets will be needed.

A plan for a simple application to pick numbers for a lottery entry might look like this:

Program purpose

● The program will generate a series of six unique random numbers in the range 1-49 and have the ability to be reset

Functionality required

● A function to generate and display six unique random numbers
● A function to clear the last six random numbers from display

Interface widgets needed

● One non-resizable window to contain all other widgets and to display the application title.
● One Label widget to display a static application logo image – just to enhance the appearance of the interface.
● Six Label widgets to dynamically display the generated series of unique random numbers – one number per Label.
● One Button widget to generate and display the numbers in the Label widgets when this Button gets clicked. This Button will not be enabled when the numbers <u>are</u> on display.
● One Button widget to clear the numbers on display in the Label widgets when this Button gets clicked. This Button will not be enabled when the numbers <u>are not</u> on display.

Having established a program plan means you can now produce the application basics by creating all the necessary widgets.

Hot tip

Toggle the value of a **Button** widget's **state** property from **NORMAL** to **DISABLED** to steer the user – in this case the application must be reset before a further series of unique random numbers can be generated.

1 Start a new program by importing all features from the "tkinter" module
```
# Widgets:
from tkinter import *
```

2 Next, add statements to create a window object and an image object
```
window = Tk()
img = PhotoImage( file = 'lotto.gif' )
```

lotto(widgets).py

3 Now, add statements to create all the necessary widgets
```
imgLbl = Label( window, image = img )
label1 = Label( window, relief = 'groove', width = 2 )
label2 = Label( window, relief = 'groove', width = 2 )
label3 = Label( window, relief = 'groove', width = 2 )
label4 = Label( window, relief = 'groove', width = 2 )
label5 = Label( window, relief = 'groove', width = 2 )
label6 = Label( window, relief = 'groove', width = 2 )
getBtn = Button( window )
resBtn = Button( window )
```

lotto.gif

4 Then, add the widgets to the window using the grid layout manager – ready to receive arguments to specify how the widgets should be positioned at the design stage next
```
# Geometry:
imgLbl.grid()
label1.grid()
label2.grid()
label3.grid()
label4.grid()
label5.grid()
label6.grid()
getBtn.grid()
resBtn.grid()
```

The **relief** property specifies a border style and the **width** property specifies the label width in character numbers.

5 Finally, add a loop statement to sustain the window
```
# Sustain window:
window.mainloop()
```

6 Save the file then run the program – to see the window appear containing all the necessary widgets

Designing layout

Having created all the necessary widgets, as shown on the previous page, you can now design the interface layout by adding arguments to specify how the widgets should be positioned. A horizontal design will position the logo Label on the left, and on its right all six other Labels in a row with both Buttons below this. The grid layout manager, which positions widgets in rows and columns, can easily produce this design by allowing the logo Label to span a row containing all six other Labels and also a row containing both Buttons. One Button can span four columns and the other Button can span two columns, arranged like this:

Hot tip

The grid layout manager's **rowspan** and **columnspan** properties work like the HTML **rowspan** and **colspan** table cell attributes.

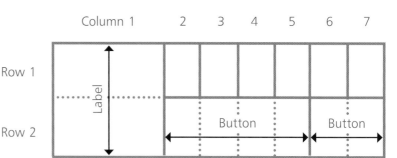

lotto(layout).py

 Edit the program started on the previous page – firstly by positioning the Label containing the logo in the first column of the first row, and have it span across the second row

```
# Geometry:
imgLbl.grid( row = 1, column = 1, rowspan = 2 )
```

2 Next, position a Label in the second column of the first row and add 10 pixels of padding to its left and right
```
label1.grid( row = 1, column = 2, padx = 10 )
```

3 Now, position a Label in the third column of the first row and add 10 pixels of padding to its left and right
```
label2.grid( row = 1, column = 3, padx = 10 )
```

 Position a Label in the fourth column of the first row and add 10 pixels of padding to its left and right
```
label3.grid( row = 1, column = 4, padx = 10 )
```

5 Position a Label in the fifth column of the first row and add 10 pixels of padding to its left and right
`label4.grid( row = 1, column = 5, padx = 10 )`

6 Position a Label in the sixth column of the first row and add 10 pixels of padding to its left and right
`label5.grid( row = 1, column = 6, padx = 10 )`

7 Position a Label in the seventh column of the first row then add 10 pixels of padding to the left side of the Label and 20 pixels of padding to the right side of the Label
`label6.grid( row = 1, column = 7, padx = ( 10, 20 ) )`

Hot tip

Additional padding to the right of the Label in the final column of the first row extends the window width to simply create a small right-hand margin area.

8 Next, position a Button in the second column of the second row and have it span across four columns
`getBtn.grid( row = 2, column = 2, columnspan = 4 )`

9 Now, position a Button in the sixth column of the second row, and have it span across two columns
`resBtn.grid( row = 2, column = 6, columnspan = 2 )`

10 Save the file then run the program – to see the window appear containing all the necessary widgets now arranged in your grid layout design

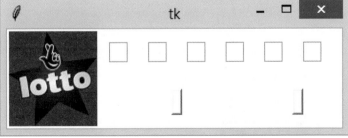

Hot tip

The Buttons will expand to fit static text that will appear on each Button face – specified in the next stage.

The window size is automatically adjusted to suit the grid contents and the Button widgets are automatically centered in the spanned column width.

163

Assigning statics

Having arranged all the necessary widgets in a grid layout, as shown on the previous page, you can now assign static values to the widgets. These values will not change during execution of the program.

lotto(static).py

 Modify the program on the previous page by inserting a new section just before the final loop statement, which begins with a statement specifying a window title
 # Static Properties:
window.title('Lotto Number Picker' **)**

 Next, add a statement to prevent the user resizing the window along both the X axis and the Y axis – this will disable the window's "resize" button
window.resizable(0, 0)

 Now, add a statement to specify text to appear on the face of the first Button widget
getBtn.configure(text = 'Get My Lucky Numbers' **)**

 Then, add a statement to specify text to appear on the face of the second Button widget
resBtn.configure(text = 'Reset' **)**

5 Save the file then execute the program – to see the window now has a title, its resize button is disabled, and the buttons have now been resized to suit their text

Hot tip

The widget's **configure()** method allows properties to be subsequently added or modified after they have been created.

Lotto Number Picker

Get My Lucky Numbers   Reset

Loading dynamics

Having specified values for static properties, as shown on the facing page, initial values can now be specified for those properties whose values <u>will</u> change dynamically during execution of the program.

1 Modify the program on the facing page by inserting another new section just before the final loop statement, which specifies that each small empty Label should initially display an ellipsis

```
# Initial Properties:
label1.configure( text = '...' )

label2.configure( text = '...' )

label3.configure( text = '...' )

label4.configure( text = '...' )

label5.configure( text = '...' )

label6.configure( text = '...' )
```

lotto(initial).py

2 Next, add a statement to specify that the second Button widget should initially be disabled

```
resBtn.configure( state = DISABLED )
```

3 Save the file then run the program – to see each small Label now displays an ellipsis and that the "Reset" Button has been disabled

Button states are recognized by **tkinter** constants of **DISABLED** (off), **NORMAL** (on), or **ACTIVE** (pressed).

Adding functionality

Having created code to initialize dynamic properties, on the previous page, you can now add runtime functionality to respond to clicks on the Button widgets during execution of the program.

lotto.py

1 Modify the program on the previous page by inserting one more new section just before the final loop statement, which begins by making the **sample()** function available from the "random" module

```
# Dynamic Properties:
from random import sample
```

2 Next, define a function that generates and assigns six unique random numbers to the small Labels and reverses the state of both Buttons

```
def pick() :
        nums = sample( range( 1, 49 ), 6 )
        label1.configure( text = nums[0] )
        label2.configure( text = nums[1] )
        label3.configure( text = nums[2] )
        label4.configure( text = nums[3] )
        label5.configure( text = nums[4] )
        label6.configure( text = nums[5] )
        getBtn.configure( state = DISABLED )
        resBtn.configure( state = NORMAL )
```

3 Now, define a function to display an ellipsis on each small Label and revert both Buttons to their initial states

```
def reset() :
        label1.configure( text = '...' )
        label2.configure( text = '...' )
        label3.configure( text = '...' )
        label4.configure( text = '...' )
        label5.configure( text = '...' )
        label6.configure( text = '...' )
        getBtn.configure( state = NORMAL )
        resBtn.configure( state = DISABLED )
```

Hot tip

These steps provide comparable functionality to that of the console application on page 159.

4 Then, add statements to nominate the relevant function to be called when each Button is pressed by the user

```
getBtn.configure( command = pick )
resBtn.configure( command = reset )
```

5 Finally, save the file – the complete program should look like that shown opposite

```
# Widgets:
from tkinter import *
window = Tk()
img = PhotoImage( file = 'lotto.gif')                    )
imgLbl = Label( window, image = img )
label1 = Label( window, relief = 'groove', width = 2 )
label2 = Label( window, relief = 'groove', width = 2 )
label3 = Label( window, relief = 'groove', width = 2 )
label4 = Label( window, relief = 'groove', width = 2 )
label5 = Label( window, relief = 'groove', width = 2 )
label6 = Label( window, relief = 'groove', width = 2 )
getBtn = Button( window )
resBtn = Button( window )

# Geometry:
imgLbl.grid( row = 1, column = 1, rowspan = 2 )
label1.grid( row = 1, column = 2, padx = 10 )
label2.grid( row = 1, column = 3, padx = 10 )
label3.grid( row = 1, column = 4, padx = 10 )
label4.grid( row = 1, column = 5, padx = 10 )
label5.grid( row = 1, column = 6, padx = 10 )
label6.grid( row = 1, column = 7, padx = ( 10, 20 ) )
getBtn.grid( row = 2, column = 2, columnspan = 4 )
resBtn.grid( row = 2, column = 6, columnspan = 2 )

# Static Properties:
window.title( 'Lotto Number Picker' )
window.resizable( 0, 0 )
getBtn.configure( text = 'Get My Lucky Numbers' )
resBtn.configure( text = 'Reset' )

# Initial Properties:
label1.configure( text = '...' )
label2.configure( text = '...' )
label3.configure( text = '...' )
label4.configure( text = '...' )
label5.configure( text = '...' )
label6.configure( text = '...' )
resBtn.configure( state = DISABLED )

# Dynamic Properties:
from random import sample

def pick() :
        nums = sample( range( 1, 49 ), 6 )
        label1.configure( text = nums[0] )
        label2.configure( text = nums[1] )
        label3.configure( text = nums[2] )
        label4.configure( text = nums[3] )
        label5.configure( text = nums[4] )
        label6.configure( text = nums[5] )
        getBtn.configure( state = DISABLED )
        resBtn.configure( state = NORMAL )

def reset() :
        label1.configure( text = '...' )
        label2.configure( text = '...' )
        label3.configure( text = '...' )
        label4.configure( text = '...' )
        label5.configure( text = '...' )
        label6.configure( text = '...' )
        getBtn.configure( state = NORMAL )
        resBtn.configure( state = DISABLED )

getBtn.configure( command = pick )
resBtn.configure( command = reset )

# Sustain window:
window.mainloop()
```

It is convention to place all **import** statements at the start of the script but they can appear anywhere, as listed here.

Testing programs

Having worked through the program plan, on the previous pages, the widgets needed and functionality required have now been added to the application – so it's ready to be tested.

 Launch the application and examine its initial appearance

Static text appears on the window title bar and on the Button widgets, the window's resize button is disabled, the small Labels contain their initial ellipsis text values, and the "Reset" button is in its initial disabled state.

 Next, click the "Get My Lucky Numbers" Button widget – to execute all the statements within the **pick()** function

Don't forget

No number is repeated in any series because the random **sample()** function returns a set of <u>unique</u> random integers.

A series of numbers within the desired range is displayed and the Button states have changed as required – a further series of numbers cannot be generated until the application has been reset.

 Make a note of the numbers generated in this first series for comparison later

...cont'd

4 Click the "Reset" Button widget – to execute all the statements within the **reset()** function and see the application resume its initial appearance as required

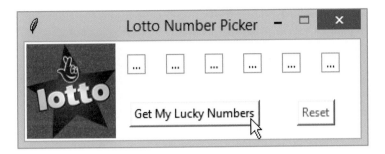

5 Click the "Get My Lucky Numbers" Button widget again – to execute its **pick()** function again and confirm that the new series of numbers differ from the first series

6 Finally, restart the application and click the "Get My Lucky Numbers" Button widget once more – and confirm that this first series of numbers are different to those noted in the first series when the application last ran

The series of generated numbers are not repeated each time the application gets launched because the random generator is seeded by the current system time – which is different each time the generator gets called.

Beware

At the time of printing, cx_Freeze for Python 3.5 is not released, but is expected soon!

Hot tip

The cx_Freeze tool can also create executable files for Mac and Linux systems. Discover more on cx_Freeze online at **cx_freeze.readthedocs.org**

setup.py

Deploying applications

Your apps developed in the Python language can be deployed on Windows systems where the Python interpreter is not installed. To do so, all the program files must be "frozen" into a bundle that includes an executable (**.exe**) file to create a simple MSI installer. The "cx_Freeze" tool is a free set of scripts and modules for freezing Python programs available at **cx-freeze.sourceforge.net**

The cx_Freeze tool uses Python's "distutils" package and requires a setup script to describe your module distribution in order to bundle appropriate support for your application. The setup script is traditionally named **setup.py** and consists mainly of a call to a cx_Freeze **setup()** function – supplying information as parameter pairs. This specifies any required build options, such as image files or modules to be included, and identifies the executable script and system platform type. For example, the setup script for the application developed throughout this chapter must include the logo image file **lotto.gif** and specify the final code script named **lotto.py** as the executable script. Once cx_Freeze is installed, a setup script can be executed from a Windows Command Prompt with the argument **bdist-msi** – to create a sub-directory named "dist" containing a distributable MSI installer for your app.

1 In IDLE start a Python setup script by making available the "sys" module and items from the "cx_Freeze" module
```
import sys
from cx_Freeze import setup, Executable
```

2 Next, add statements to identify the base platform in use
```
base = None
if sys.platform == 'win32' : base = 'Win32GUI'
```

3 Now, add a statement listing options to be included
```
opts = { 'include_files' : [ 'lotto.gif' ] , 'includes' : [ 're' ] }
```

4 Finally, add a call to the **setup()** function passing all information as parameter pairs
```
setup(  name = 'Lotto' ,
        version = '1.0' ,
        description = 'Lottery Number Picker' ,
        author = 'Mike McGrath' ,
        options = { 'build_exe' : opts } ,
        executables = [ Executable( 'lotto.py', base= base ) ] )
```

Save the setup script alongside the application files then run the script command to create the Windows installer

```
Command Prompt - python  setup.py bdist_msi          –  □  ×

C:\MyCode\Lotto>python setup.py bdist_msi
running bdist_msi
running build
running build_exe
```

Lotto-1.0-win32.msi

Wait until the process creates the installer in a "dist" sub-directory then copy the installer onto portable media, such as a USB flash drive

Now, copy the installer onto another Windows computer where Python may not be present and run the installer

Then, select an installation location, or accept the suggested default location

```
Lotto Setup                    ×

Select destinaton directory          Lotto Setup                    ×

                              Install Lotto
Lotto
                              Please wait while the installer installs Lotto.

                              Status:  Copying new files

```

lotto.exe

When the installer has finished copying files, navigate to your chosen installation location and run the executable file – to see the application launch

Summary

- The standard Python library has a **random** module that provides functions to generate pseudo-random numbers

- A pseudo-random floating-point number from 0.0 to 1.0 can be generated by the **random** module's **random()** function

- Multiple unique random integers within a given range can be generated by the **random** module's **sample()** function

- A program plan should define the program's Purpose, required Functionality, and the Interface widgets needed

- In designing a program interface the **grid()** layout manager positions widgets in rows and columns

- Static properties <u>do not</u> change during execution of a program

- Dynamic properties <u>do</u> change during execution of a program using runtime functionality to respond to a user action

- Upon completion, a program should be tested to ensure it performs as expected in every respect

- Program files can be "frozen" into a bundle for distribution to other computers where the Python interpreter is not present

- The cx_Freeze tool uses Python's "distutils" package to freeze programs into executables for Windows, Mac, or Linux

- A setup script describes your module distribution so cx_Freeze will bundle appropriate support for the application

- Traditionally, a setup script is named **setup.py** and consists mainly of a call to the cx_Freeze setup() function

- Applications can be deployed on Windows systems using the cx_Freeze tool to create a simple installer

- When a setup script is executed with the **bdist_msi** command an MSI installer is created that will copy the distribution bundle onto the host computer, including an executable file

13 Transferring skills

This chapter demonstrates similarities and differences in coding various popular programming languages.

Understanding compilers

Modern apps are coded in "high-level" languages that provide a high level of abstraction between machine code, which is understood by computers, and source code that is human-readable. In order to run programs the source code must first be rendered into machine code that the computer can execute. This process is accomplished either by an "interpreter" or by a "compiler" depending upon the language in which the program is written.

The Python programming language, used for demonstration throughout the previous chapters of this book, uses an interpreter to translate program source code. As a program proceeds, the interpreter dynamically translates its functions and statement code objects into "bytecode". The bytecode can then be executed via Python's bytecode interpreter (a.k.a. "Virtual Machine" or "VM").

Other programming languages that employ an interpreter to translate source code into bytecode for execution by the computer via their virtual machine include Java and Ruby.

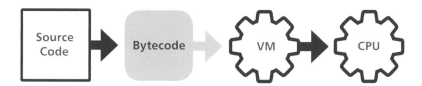

Traditional programming languages, such as the C language, use a compiler to convert program source code into machine code. Compilation takes the entire source code and first generates intermediate "object code" representing the program's functions and statements in binary machine code format. The compiler then combines the object code into a single binary machine code file (.exe) that can be executed directly by the computer.

Other programming languages that employ a compiler to convert source code into machine code for direct execution by the computer include C++ ("C plus plus") and C# ("C sharp").

Hot tip

Often languages that employ an interpreter are referred to as "interpreted languages" and those that use a compiler are referred to as "compiled languages".

Don't forget

Notice that the Virtual Machine (VM) must be present on the user's computer to execute those programs written in interpreted languages.

There are, therefore, fundamental differences in the way programs written in "interpreted languages", such as Python, and "compiled languages" such as the C language, are executed by the computer. Each offers some advantages and disadvantages in terms of performance and portability, as listed in the table below:

Interpreter:	Compiler:
Takes individual code objects as input for *translation*	Takes the entire source code as input for *conversion*
Does not generate intermediate object code	*Does* generate intermediate object code
Executes conditional control statements *slowly*	Executes conditional control statements *quickly*
Requires *little* memory as object code is not generated	Requires *more* memory as object code is generated
Translates the source code *every time* the program runs	Converts the source code *once* during compilation
Reports any errors *immediately* when they occur in a statement	Reports any errors only *after* an attempt to compile the entire source code
Programs run *slower* while code objects get individually translated to machine code	Programs run *faster* while machine code runs directly on the computer
Distributed programs are human-readable source code so are *easy* to modify	Distributed programs are compiled machine code so are *difficult* to modify
Offers *poorer* protection of intellectual property rights	Offers *better* protection of intellectual property rights

Beware

Don't be confused by Java programs. They are "compiled" into bytecode as a distributable (.class) file that nonetheless require the Java VM bytecode interpreter to run.

Compiling code

To more fully understand the compilation process it is useful to examine in detail the compilation of a simple C language program. In producing an executable file from an original C source code file the compilation process actually undergoes four separate stages, which each generate a new file:

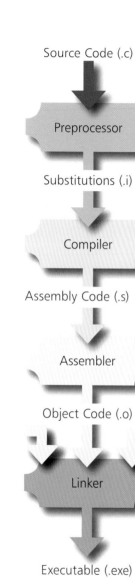

Source Code (.c)

Preprocessor

Substitutions (.i)

Compiler

Assembly Code (.s)

Assembler

Object Code (.o)

Linker

Executable (.exe)

- **Preprocessing** – the preprocessor stage first substitutes all "preprocessor" directives, such as statements to import libraries, with the actual library code. For instance, in the C language the library code is substituted for **#include** import directives. The generated file containing the substitutions is in text format and typically has a **.i** file extension

- **Translating** – the compiler stage translates the high-level instructions in the .i file into low-level Assembly language instructions. The generated file containing the translation is in text format and typically has a **.s** file extension

- **Assembling** – the assembler stage converts the Assembly language text instructions in the **.s** file into machine code. The generated object file containing the conversion is in binary format and typically has a **.o** file extension

- **Linking** – the linker stage combines one or more binary object **.o** files into a single executable file. The generated file is in binary format and typically has a **.exe** file extension

Strictly speaking, "compilation" describes the first three stages above, which operate on a single source code text file and ultimately generate a single binary object file. Where the program source code contains syntax errors, such as a missing statement terminator or a missing parenthesis, they will be reported by the compiler and compilation will fail.

The linker, on the other hand, can operate on multiple object files and ultimately generates a single executable file. This allows the creation of large programs from modular object files that may each contain re-usable functions. Where the linker finds a function of the same name defined in multiple object files it will report an error and the executable file will not be created.

...cont'd

Normally, the temporary files created during the intermediary stages of the compilation process are automatically deleted, but the GNU C Compiler (gcc) provides a **-save-temps** option in the compiler command that allows them to be saved for inspection.

For a simple "Hello World!" program in the C language, type a command **gcc hello.c -save-temps -o hello.exe** then hit Return to compile and save the temporary files

Hot tip

In the command here, **gcc** invokes the compiler, the source code file is **hello.c**, and **-o hello.exe** specifies the executable file to be output.

Open the **hello.i** file in a plain text editor, such as Windows' Notepad, to see the source code appear at the very end of the file – preceded by substituted library code

3 Now, open the **hello.s** file in a plain text editor to see the translation into low-level Assembly code and note how unfriendly that appears in contrast to high-level code

Hot tip

A complete example demonstrating how to code and compile programs in the C programming language is provided overleaf.

177

Coding C

The coding data structures and control structures described and demonstrated throughout this book in the Python programming language also exist in other programming languages. Your skills gained with Python coding can be transferred to other languages, such as the C programming language, by recognizing similarities. The C programming language originated way back in the 1970s and is designed to be easily compiled to low-level machine code. Its efficiency makes it suitable for a wide range of applications in everything from embedded systems to operating systems.

The simple Guessing Game program, described in Python code on pages 30 and 31, can be recreated in a similar C equivalent.

guess.c

1 Start a new C program by importing libraries to make input-output, random number, and time functions available
```
#include <stdio.h>
#include <stdlib.h>
#include <time.h>
```

2 Next, define a "main" function body that will enclose the entire game code and return a zero value on completion
```
int main( )
{
  /* Statements to be added here */
  return 0 ;
}
```

3 Now, add statements to initialize variables with a random number in the range 1-20, a Boolean true, and an integer
```
srand( time( NULL ) ) ;
int num = ( rand() % 20 ) + 1 ;
int flag = 1 ;
int guess = 0 ;
```

Beware

This C program will accept floating-point guesses as their value gets truncated to an integer in the assignment to the **guess** variable.

4 Add a statement to request user input
```
printf( "Guess my number 1-20 : " ) ;
```

5 Then, add a loop statement that reads input into the integer variable and will enclose a conditional test
```
while ( flag == 1 )
{
  scanf( "%d" , &guess ) ; fflush( stdin ) ;
  /* Conditional test to be added here */
}
```

6 Finally, add a conditional test inside the loop then save, compile, and run the program

```c
if( guess == 0 )
{
  printf( "Invalid! Enter only digits 1-20\n" ) ;
  break ;
}
else if ( guess < num ) { printf( "Too low, try again : " ) ; }
else if ( guess > num ) { printf( "Too high,try again : " ) ; }
else
{
  printf( "Correct... My number is %d \n" , num ) ;
  flag = 0 ;
}
```

```
Command Prompt                                    _ □ ×

C:\MyCode>gcc guess.c -o guess.exe

C:\MyCode>guess
Guess my number 1-20 : ten
Invalid! Enter only digits 1-20

C:\MyCode>guess
Guess my number 1-20 : 10
Too high,try again : 2
Too low, try again : 5
Correct... My number is 5

C:\MyCode>_
```

The GNU C Compiler (gcc) is widely used and is freely available as part of the Minimalist GNU for Windows (MinGW) package from **sourceforge.net/ projects/mingw** For installation instructions and other help refer to the documentation at **mingw.org/wiki**

Guessing Game in C – program comparison

- Library functions are made available in C programs with an **#include** directive, like using Python's **import** keyword

- C programs always have a **main()** function that gets called automatically whenever the program runs

- Statements in C programs are grouped inside **{ }** braces

- Variables in C are not loosely typed so their data type, such as **int** (integer), must be defined in their declaration

- The end of each statement in C must be denoted with a ; semi-colon character – tabs and spaces are irrelevant

- Control structures in C programs use **if** , **else**, and **while** keywords – in much the same way as Python programs

Coding C++

The coding data structures and control structures described and demonstrated throughout this book in the Python programming language also exist in the C++ programming language. Your skills gained with Python coding can be transferred to that language by recognizing its similarities to Python code. The C++ programming language originated back in the 1980s as an enhancement of the C language, known as "C with classes". These classes define programming objects that transform the procedural nature of C for object-oriented programming in C++.

The simple Guessing Game program, described in Python code on pages 30 and 31, can be recreated in a similar C++ equivalent.

guess.cpp

1 Start a new C++ program by importing libraries to make input-output, random number, and time functions available
```
#include <iostream>
#include <cstdlib>
#include <ctime>
```

2 Next, define a "main" function body that will enclose the entire game code and return a zero value on completion
```
int main( )
{
  /* Statements to be added here */
  return 0 ;
}
```

3 Now, add statements to initialize variables with a random number in the range 1-20, a Boolean true, and an integer
```
srand( time( 0 ) ) ;
int num = ( rand() % 20 ) + 1 ;
bool flag = true ;
int guess = 0 ;
```

4 Add a statement to request user input
```
std::cout << "Guess my number 1-20 : " ;
```

5 Then, add a loop statement that reads input into the integer variable and will enclose a conditional test
```
while ( flag == 1 )
{
  std::cin >> guess ; std::cin.ignore( 256 , '\n' ) ;
  /* Conditional test to be added here */
}
```

Beware

This C++ program will accept floating-point guesses as their value gets truncated to an integer in the assignment to the **guess** variable.

6 Finally, add a conditional test inside the loop then save, compile, and run the program

```cpp
if( guess == 0 ) {
  std::cout << "Invalid! Enter only digits 1-20\n" ;
  break ;
}
else if ( guess < num ) {
  std::cout << "Too low, try again : " ; }
else if ( guess > num ) {
  std::cout << "Too high,try again : " ; }
else {
  std::cout << "Correct... My number is " << num << "\n" ;
  flag = 0 ;
}
```

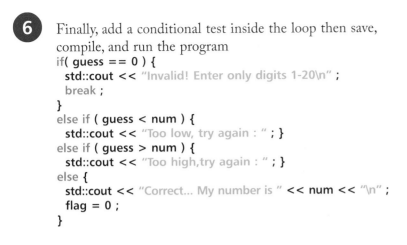

```
C:\MyCode>c++ guess.cpp -o guessplus.exe

C:\MyCode>guessplus
Guess my number 1-20 : ten
Invalid! Enter only digits 1-20

C:\MyCode>guessplus
Guess my number 1-20 : 10
Too low, try again : 18
Too high,try again : 16
Correct... My number is 16

C:\MyCode>_
```

The Minimalist GNU for Windows (MinGW) package from **sourceforge.net/ projects/mingw** also optionally provides a compiler for C++ code. In the command here **c++** invokes the compiler, the source code file is **guess.cpp**, and **-o guessplus.exe** specifies the executable file to be output.

Guessing Game in C++ – program comparison

- Library functions are made available in C++ programs with an **#include** directive, like using Python's **import** keyword

- C++ programs always have a **main()** function that gets called automatically whenever the program runs

- Statements in C++ programs are grouped inside **{ }** braces

- Variables in C++ are not loosely typed so their data type, such as **int** (integer), must be defined in their declaration

- The end of each statement in C++ must be denoted with a ; semi-colon character – tabs and spaces are irrelevant

- Control structures in C++ programs use **if, else,** and **while** keywords – in much the same way as Python programs

Coding C#

The coding data structures and control structures described and demonstrated throughout this book in the Python programming language also exist in the C# programming language. Your skills gained with Python coding can be transferred to that language by recognizing its similarities to Python code. The C# programming language was developed by Microsoft for its .NET initiative. Programs in C# require the Common Language Runtime (CLR) to be installed on the host computer to produce machine code at runtime – a process known as "Just-In-Time" (JIT) compilation.

The simple Guessing Game program, described in Python code on pages 30 and 31, can be recreated in a similar C# equivalent.

guess.cs

Hot tip

This C# program will not accept floating-point guesses as they are intelligently recognized as non-integers by the **int.TryParse()** function.

1 Start a new C# program by importing the namespace to make input-output and random number functions available
using **System** ;

2 Next, define a class structure to enclose the entire game code within a "Main" function
class **Guess**
{
  static void **Main( )**
  {
    /* Statements to be added here */
  }
} ;

3 Now, add statements to initialize variables with a random number in the range 1-20, a Boolean true, and an integer
Random generator = new Random( ) ;
int **num** = generator.Next(1 , 20 + 1) ;
bool **flag** = true ;
int **guess** = 0 ;

4 Add a statement to request user input
Console.WriteLine("Guess my number 1-20 : ") ;

5 Then, add a loop statement that reads input into the integer variable and will enclose a conditional test
while (**flag** == true)
{
  int.TryParse(Console.ReadLine( ) , out **guess**) ;
  /* Conditional test to be added here */
}

6 Finally, add a conditional test inside the loop then save, compile, and run the program

```csharp
if( guess == 0 ) {
  Console.Write( "Invalid! Enter only digits 1-20\n" ) ;
  break ;
}
else if ( guess < num ) {
  Console.Write( "Too low, try again : " ) ; }
else if ( guess > num ) {
  Console.Write( "Too high,try again : " ) ; }
else {
  Console.Write( "Correct... My number is " + num + "\n" ) ;
  flag = false ;
}
```

```
C:\                   Command Prompt              –  □  ×

C:\MyCode>csc /out:guesssharp.exe guess.cs

C:\MyCode>guesssharp
Guess my number 1-20 : ten
Invalid! Enter only digits 1-20

C:\MyCode>guesssharp
Guess my number 1-20 : 10
Too low, try again : 18
Too high,try again : 12
Correct... My number is 12

C:\MyCode>_
```

The Visual Studio Community IDE is a great development environment for C# programming. It is available free from **visualstudio.com** and includes the C Sharp Compiler (**csc.exe**). In the command here **csc** invokes the compiler, **/out: guesssharp.exe** specifies the executable file to be output, and the source code file is named **guess.cs**.

183

Guessing Game in C# – program comparison

- Library functions are made available in C# programs with a **using** directive, like using Python's **import** keyword

- C# programs always have a class structure enclosing a **Main()** function that gets called automatically when the program runs

- Statements in C# programs are grouped inside **{ }** braces

- Variables in C# are not loosely typed so their data type, such as **bool** (Boolean), must be defined in their declaration

- The end of each statement in C# must be denoted with a ; semi-colon character – tabs and spaces are irrelevant

- Control structures in C# programs use **if**, **else**, and **while** keywords – in much the same way as Python programs

Coding Java

The coding data structures and control structures described and demonstrated throughout this book in the Python programming language also exist in the Java programming language. Your skills gained with Python coding can be transferred to that language by recognizing its similarities to Python code. The Java programming language has the admirable mantra "write once – run anywhere". Programs in Java require the Java Runtime Environment (JRE) to be installed on the host computer to produce machine code at runtime – a process known as "Just-In-Time" (JIT) compilation.

The simple Guessing Game program, described in Python code on pages 30 and 31, can be recreated in a similar Java equivalent.

Guess.java

 1 Start a new Java program by defining a class structure to enclose the entire game code within a "main" function

```java
class Guess
{
  public static void main( String[ ] args )
  {
    /* Statements to be added here */
  }
} ;
```

2 Now, add statements to initialize variables with a random number in the range 1-20, a Boolean true, and an integer

```java
int num = ( int ) ( Math.random( ) * 20 + 1 ) ;
boolean flag = true ;
int guess = 0 ;
```

3 Add a statement to request user input

```java
System.out.print( "Guess my number 1-20 : " ) ;
```

 4 Then, add a loop statement that reads input into the integer variable and will enclose a conditional test

```java
while ( flag == true )
{
  try {
  guess = Integer.parseInt( System.console().readLine() ) ; }
  catch ( NumberFormatException ex ) { }

  /* Conditional test to be added here */
}
```

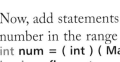

Hot tip

This Java program will not accept floating-point guesses as they are recognized as non-integers by the function **Integer.parseInt( )**.

5 Finally, add a conditional test inside the loop then save, compile, and run the program

```
if( guess == 0 ) {
  System.out.println( "Invalid! Enter only digits 1-20" ) ;
  break ;
}
else if ( guess < num ) {
  System.out.print( "Too low, try again : " ) ; }
else if ( guess > num ) {
  System.out.print( "Too high,try again : " ) ; }
else {
  System.out.println( "Correct... My number is " + num ) ;
  flag = false ;
}
```

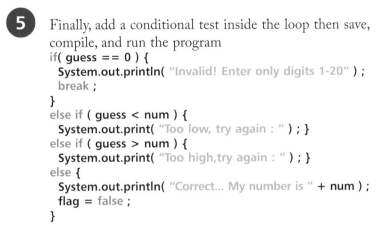

```
Command Prompt                              _ □ ×

C:\MyCode>javac Guess.java

C:\MyCode>java Guess
Guess my number 1-20 : ten
Invalid! Enter only digits 1-20

C:\MyCode>java Guess
Guess my number 1-20 : 10
Too high, try again : 2
Too low, try again : 3
Correct... My number is 3

C:\MyCode>_
```

The Java Development Kit (JDK) is needed to create Java programs. It is available free from **oracle.com** and includes the command-line Java Compiler (**javac.exe**). In the command here **javac** invokes the compiler for **Guess.java** source code and will automatically output an executable file named **Guess.exe**. This can then be run by the JRE using the **java** command.

Guessing Game in Java – program comparison

● Input-output and random number functions are readily available in Java programs without **import** statements

● Java programs always have a class structure enclosing a **main()** function that gets called automatically when the program runs

● Statements in Java programs are grouped inside **{ }** braces

● Variables in Java are not loosely typed so their data type, such as **boolean**, must be defined in their declaration

● The end of each statement in Java must be denoted with a **;** semi-colon character – tabs and spaces are irrelevant

● Control structures in Java programs use **if**, **else**, and **while** keywords – in much the same way as Python programs

Summary

- Modern programming languages, like Python or C, provide a high level of abstraction from low level machine code
- Human-readable high-level source code can be rendered into low-level machine code by an interpreter or by a compiler
- Interpreted programming languages, such as Python, translate source code into bytecode, which can then be executed via their Virtual Machine bytecode interpreter
- Compiled programming languages, such as C, generate intermediate object code that gets combined into machine code, which can then be executed directly on the computer
- The compilation of a C program translates high-level source code into low-level Assembly language then machine code
- Intermediate files generated during the compilation process are normally deleted automatically by the compiler
- The data structures and control structures used in Python also exist in the C, C++, C#, and Java programming languages – so programming skills are transferrable across languages
- Compiled programming languages, such as C, have a main function that is called automatically when the program runs
- Statements in many programming languages are grouped within { } braces and must end with a ; semi-colon
- Programming languages that have strongly typed variables require the data type that the variable may contain, such as **int** integer, to be defined in the variable declaration
- Like Python, other programming languages can also import functionality from their libraries
- C# programs require the Common Language Runtime (CLR) to be installed to produce machine code at runtime
- Java programs require the Java Runtime Environment (JRE) to be installed to produce machine code at runtime

Index

U

V

W

Z